3.9-47

THE ANTIPOETRY
OF
NICANOR PARRA

The publication of this work has been made possible by assis-
tance from the Center for Inter-American Relations, the
Andrew W. Mellon Foundation, and Dominican College of
Blauvelt.

THE ANTIPOETRY
OF
NICANOR PARRA

Edith Grossman

New York: NEW YORK UNIVERSITY PRESS

Library of Congress Catalog Card Number: 74-21609

ISBN: 0-8147-2958-4

Library of Congress Cataloging in Publication Data
Grossman, Edith, 1936-
  The antipoetry of Nicanor Parra.
  Bibliography: p.
  1. Parra, Nicanor, 1914-   —Technique.
I. Title.
PQ 8097.P322Z63   861   74-21609
ISBN 0-8147-2958-4

Manufactured in the United States of America

Preface

Nicanor Parra, one of the most important poets in Latin America today, is the originator of antipoetry. This crucial exploration of poetic diction, statement and style in the Spanish language shares in the contemporary tendency to create art where it did not exist before—to forge it from the elements of ordinary experience once considered indecorous, unartful and ugly. Antipoetry is a kind of verbalized found art that uses ordinary objects and commonplace language, colors them with a sometimes mordant, often comic irony and views them in a decidedly unexpected way. Clichés, receding hairlines and toothbrushes, for example, and we who suffer them with varying degrees of rebellion or resignation, are the stuff of Parra's sardonic and essentially moralizing commentary on the nature of man and all his works.

The antipoetic style grows out of Parra's affirmation of the fundamental unity of language, his conviction that antipoetry can span and thereby negate the artificial and unnecessary distance which separates a "real" from a "poetic" idiom. His effort has been to force poetry out of what he calls "literary space" and into "real space" where the reader and the poet can share an intensely felt response to familiar realities. He has tried to strip poetry's language bare, but not for the sake of what he would consider élitist purity of diction. On the contrary, he has cherished the prosaic quality and fumbling hesitation of ordinary, unprepared speech because it is "impure," because it has profound expressive and ironic possibilities and a unique capacity for rendering simultaneous bathos and tragedy. In the process of what is, to the antipoet's mind, a salutory reduction of poetic language to its most simple common denominator, he has perfected a complex poetic structure that obliges the reader to first perceive and then participate, almost against his will, in the frequently comic despair of the antipoetic protagonist. Parra's honed treatment of familiar experience, what he calls the "galvanization" of the reader into a new and perhaps uncomfortable recognition of his own circumstances, depends on the poetic persona as the intermediary for the confrontation, but between the reader and his own, newly revealed reality Parra refuses to erect rhetorical, metaphorical or imagistic barriers. The antipoet considers them superfluous or "poetic." Parra's sense of himself as the antipoet demands that he

reunite the poetic art and its natural audience, too
long and painfully separated by what he deems pur-
poseful obscurity and artificial diction. In other
words, if poetry does not communicate, then antipoetry will; if poetry no longer moves its readers to
responsiveness, then antipoetry will.

Parra fears for the future of poetry, and his purpose as antipoet (in this sense really the pro-poet) is to
preserve poetry as a viable art form in a mass-
educated, urbanized society. His method is to create
the appearance of ordinary, spontaneous speech—the
language of the street corner, the living room,
the office—while he involves the reader directly in
the complex organization of the antipoem.

Despite Parra's importance to Latin American literature, his pioneering role in the creation of a new
kind of language for poetry in Spanish, and his close
ties with North American and English poets, there
are no book-length studies in English of his poetic
style. I hope to begin to fill the gap for the English-
speaking reader by documenting and analyzing
Parra's distinctive use of colloquial language, the
characteristic irony and burlesque that color his
writing, the specific emotive effects which he creates
out of the flat prosaic tones of his linguistic raw material and the artistic commitments which nourish
these techniques.

Parra's statements about his work reveal an urgent
sense of renovatory mission, as if he were mandated
to save poetry from itself, but a precise definition of
the intentionally provocative term antipoetry is not

to be found in his own comments on his writing. The search for such an explanation leads to a self-contradictory tangle. Parra himself has said that he chose the term antipoetry for purely "strategic reasons." He calls his work a "professional secret" and adroitly holds insistent questioners at bay: "If you put me up against the wall and say 'OK, tell us once and for all what antipoetry is,' I'll tell you I haven't the slightest idea—go ahead, frisk me."[1] With caveats like these even the most intrepid critic must pause to wonder if attempts to describe and define antipoetry will only end in ignominious disaster. The most casual comparison of Parra's remarks in interviews, at poetry readings, seminars, conferences, during informal conversations, inevitably leads back to his own formulation: "The antipoet reserves the right to make contradictory formulations."[2] And indeed, what Parra says about himself and his writing seems to change according to whim, or possibly according to what he thinks will most distract his audience. To avoid the danger of taking the wrong statement too seriously, or the right one not seriously enough, and because what a writer *does* is almost always more in-

1. Patricio Lerzundi, "In Defense of Antipoetry: An Interview with Nicanor Parra," tr. Tom J. Lewis, *Review* (Winter 1971/Spring 1972), pp. 65–72. Subsequent references will be included in the text.

2. All of Parra's statements, unless otherwise noted, were made in the seminar on antipoetry which he conducted at New York University in the summer of 1971. Subsequent references will be included in the text.

teresting and informative than what he *says* he is doing, I have included and discussed a good number
of Parra's remarks about his work in the first section of the book, but in the analytic chapters I have
concentrated on the antipoems as the most reliable
source of definitions and postulations concerning
antipoetry.

English translations of many of Parra's poems
composed since 1938 are most readily available in the
two bilingual volumes published by New Directions:
Poems and Antipoems (New York: New Directions,
1967) and *Emergency Poems* (New York: New Directions, 1972). However, I have used my own English
versions of Parra's poems in this study. They are not
meant to be poems in English, but rather prose ren-
derings of the texts which attempt to approximate
Parra's language as closely as possible. I have followed the original verse and stanzaic organization in
order to facilitate comparison with the Spanish texts
which are included in the appendix. I am responsible
for the translations of remarks originally made by
Parra in Spanish at poetry readings, in interviews
and in the seminar he taught at New York University. I also translated the excerpts from magazines,
newspapers and books originally published in Spanish. However, Parra spoke in English at O'Shea Intermediate School in New York City, and the Lerzundi
interview was published in English.

Finally, I would like to express deep and sincere
thanks to Alexander Coleman, of New York University,

who introduced me to Nicanor Parra and his work, to
Sheera Dale Stern, whose comments and suggestions
were invaluable to me, and to Ronald Christ of the
Center for Inter-American Relations, without whose
help and encouragement this book would never have
been written.

Edith Grossman

Contents

Introduction

Reading Edith Grossman's keen, succinct study of the
antipoetic principles of the Chilean poet Nicanor
Parra, I was reminded of a happy occasion that took
place in New York in Greenwich Village just a few
years ago—a public reading by Parra, with translations boisterously delivered by Allen Ginsberg. Parra
somehow lost his sly Latin subterfuges and got
transformed into purest Newyorkese, a street poet
for our day and time, schooled in subway graffiti and

subliterate remarks. It seemed that Parra had (with Ginsberg's aid, of course) jumped out of his Chilean skin and had become another loquacious and disenchanted taxi driver of poetry—feisty, pugnacious, a destructor and inventor of a mode that has nothing to do with what most people consider to be "poetry."

Parra's campaign against the idea of "poetry" makes him into a literary poujadist; a needler too, a trasher of idols who gleefully spoofs Mallarmé's hermeticism, who deflates Eliot's Christian postures, who jokes with Neruda's bardic rumblings. This onslaught includes attacks against the idea of "masterpieces" and the attendant sacralization of poetry. For Parra, the history of poetry is the history of esthetic totemization, where noble tonalities ally themselves with sacerdotal distance, where "God and the imagination are one," as Stevens would have it. A born enemy of monumentality, Parra must be the greatest literary know-nothing of all time.

The results of this fantastic program are evident in the second chapter of Ms. Grossman's study, where this scorched earth policy becomes an organic part of poems representing his unique *ars poetica*. It is, as she points out there and in other pages of her study, a subversive mechanism designed to liquidate the hieratic tone from poetry, along with its attendant metaphors, inflated diction, romantic yearning and empty nobility—not to mention the idea of the poet as hero with blinding faith in the people. "I always associated Poetry with the voice of the priest in the pulpit," he says. Poets sing, he maintains, but man talks. "Let the birds do the singing." If everyone has recognized the existence of poetry over the centuries, why not speak of "antipoetry," just as the theoretical physicist that Parra is in real life will speak of antimatter or the theory of complementarity? "Why not?" is Parra's only answer to all estheticist queries.

For Parra, there has always been a Goliard poet, a Villon, a Corbière or a Brecht to take poetry back out onto the streets. It's a long way from Olympus. This traversal back to the commonplace and the ordinary makes use of special weapons: irony, burlesque, an astringent barrage of clichés and found phrases, all juxtaposed in a welter of diction levels. Singularly, each element of an antipoem is nothing; as welded together by Parra, the antielements cohere into an antipoem which reorders our idea of literature and the "literate" act.

All the same, Edith Grossman is careful to point out the coherence behind this apparent chaos—Parra's is a mind of philosophical and even religious resonance, all coexisting in a world of comic deflation. A Chilean priest fell into Parra's trap by affirming that his poetry was "too dirty to be immoral. A garbage can isn't immoral no matter how much we poke through its contents." The good Padre Salvatierra! If he knew with what relish Parra savours *that* description, would he ever have made it? Probably not, but for Nicanor, that fulmination guarantees to Parra the only existant crown of plastic laurels.

Edith Grossman's study gives us a coherent critical and intuitive overview of Parra's theory and practice.

It is the first substantive examination of Parra's genius in any language, and I suspect will lead to a reevaluation of Parra's esthetic deviancy. Who knows, this book also may well lead poets in English to reconsider their own ideas about the nature of poetry. In any case, Parra has rankled enough sensibilities in the Hispanic world; thanks to Edith Grossman, it's now our turn to examine and consider this well-argued case for antipoetry and its existence.

ALEXANDER COLEMAN
Associate Professor
of Spanish and Portuguese
New York University

Biographical Note

Nicanor Parra was born in Chillán, a small town in southern Chile, in 1914. He published his first book of poems in 1937, *Cancionero sin nombre* (Untitled Songs), and was awarded the Premio Municipal de Poesía (Municipal Poetry Prize) in 1938. In the same year he completed his studies of mathematics and physics at the Instituto Pedagógico (Pedagogical Institute) of the University of Chile in Santiago and taught in secondary school until 1943. From 1943 to 1945 he lived in the United States, studying advanced mechanics at Brown University, and in 1948 he was appointed Director of the School of Engineering at the University of Chile. The following year he received a grant from the British Council to study cosmology at Oxford University, where he remained for two years. Parra returned to Chile in 1952 and was

named Professor of Theoretical Physics at the
University, a position which he has held since that
time. *Poemas y antipoemas* (Poems and Antipoems)
was published in 1954 and awarded the Premio del
Sindicato de Escritores (Writers' Union Prize) in 1954
and the Premio Municipal in 1955. He published *La
cueca larga* (The Long Cueca: the cueca is a native
Chilean dance) in 1958, and in 1960 selections from
Poemas y antipoemas were included in Lawrence
Ferlinghetti's City Lights Pocket Poet series. *Versos
de salón* (Salon Verses) and *Discursos* (Speeches) appeared in 1962; the latter was coauthored with Pablo
Neruda. The following year Parra was invited to the
Soviet Union, where he spent six months supervising
the translation into Spanish of an anthology of Soviet
poets, and then visited the People's Republic of China.
In 1966 he was Visiting Professor at Louisiana State
University, and in 1967 he published *Canciones rusas*
(Russian Songs). In the same year New Directions
included selections from *Poemas y antipoemas, Versos de salón, Canciones rusas* and "Ejercicios respiratorios" (Breathing Exercises, a collection not published previously in book form) in the volume *Poems
and Antipoems*. His selected works appeared in 1969
with the title *Obra gruesa* (Basic Work). The book was
awarded the Premio Nacional de Literatura (National
Literary Prize) and includes all of his previously
published volumes (except *Cancionero sin nombre*
and *Discursos*) and three groups of poems called "La
camisa de fuerza" (The Straitjacket), "Otros poemas"
(Other Poems) and "Tres poemas" (Three Poems).

Twenty-nine poems chosen from these three collections, eleven selections from an unpublished manuscript entitled "Routine and Emergency Poems" and twenty of Parra's most recent compositions were published in 1972 as *Emergency Poems*. Parra began publishing the short, aphoristic, experimental works called *artefactos* (artifacts) in 1967, and a number of them appeared in various magazines throughout Latin America. In 1972 he published them as the texts for a boxed collection of post cards—a kind of anti-book entitled *Artefactos*. In 1971 Parra was Visiting Professor at New York, Columbia and Yale Universities. He currently resides at La Reina, outside of Santiago de Chile.

NO ME CONFORMO CON LA VI(U)DA
del profesor universitario

hubiera sido preferible
ser simple hijo de familia
con palacete en la Alameda
más viajero que viñatero
claro que sin guantes pato

o senador de la república
premio lenin y premio nobel
eso sí que sin mascarones
de proa virgen del carmen

hasta la viuda miserable
del vendedor ambulante
en los puebluchos del sur
claro que sin yerno turco
tiene sus pros y sus contras

pero nací condenado
a cargar de día y de noche
el cadáver de Galileo
por los jardines del pedagógico

miren estoy más inclinado
que la propia torre de pisa

qué formidable hubiera sido
salir del país a los 20
para no volver nunca más
(el Cholo la supo hacer)
o llegar a Valparaísa
con un maletín de gásfiter
a fines del siglo pasado
hablando nicaragüense

¡yo debiera haberme casado
con una viuda millonaria
experta en zurcir calcetines!

nada de eso sucedió
y me tengo que conformar
con el pizarrón y la tiza
la tiza y el pizarrón
hasta que jubile o reviente

Nicanor Parra

I AM NOT RESIGNED TO THE W/LIFE
of the university professor

it would have been better
to be a rich man's son
with a mansion on the Alameda
a traveler not a toiler
but without the fine gloves

or a national senator
lenin prize and nobel prize
but definitely without the figureheads
mother of god!

even the poor wife
of the peddler working his way
through miserable southern villages
but without the turkish son-in-law
has her pros and cons

but I was doomed at birth
to spend my days and nights
carrying the corpse of Galileo
through pedagogical gardens

look I'm leaning even more
than the tower of pisa

how terrific it would have been
to leave the country at 20
and never return again
(Cholo managed to do it)
or to arrive in Valparaíso
at the end of the last century
carrying a plumber's satchel
and talking nicaraguan

I certainly should have married
a widow with all her millions
an expert at darning socks!

it didn't turn out that way
and I have to resign myself
to the blackboard and the chalk
the chalk and the blackboard
until I retire or die

This is the first time the poem has appeared in print. Nicanor Parra has graciously offered it for publication to serve as an introduction to this volume. (Translated by Edith Grossman.)

THE ANTIPOETRY
OF
NICANOR PARRA

CHAPTER I

The Trajectory
of Antipoetry

Nicanor Parra has been a poet for most of his life and a confessed antipoet since 1954, when he rocked the Latin American literary world with *Poemas y antipoemas*. The book definitively established him as a significant and influential writer, one who had, according to Pablo Neruda, "vanquished the sigh and was quite capable of supervising the decapitation of the sigher." [1] Parra's own semiserious version of the origins of antipoetry focuses on what he calls his three moments of "poetic illumination." The first inspired him at the age of eleven to compose an epic trilogy that recounted the history of the Araucano

1. Antonio Skarmeta, "El apogeo del antipoeta," *Ercilla* (1971), 34-39, p. 35. This issue is not available for consultation, and I cannot provide further bibliographical information. Subsequent references will be included in the text.

1

Indians, the Spaniards and the Chileans. The heroic impetus weakened before the ambitious project was completed, but he wrote other verses, alternating between dramatic national themes and a style and language so intensely sentimental that he could move his mother to tears with his poems.[2] He stopped writing during his early adolescence but in the fifth year of secondary school he composed "some poems with love, rocks and waves, comparing the waves to women, and all of it was pseudo-problematical, because I had no problems with women" (Morales, p. 171).

These juvenile compositions are not intrinsically important, but they did serve to shape his self-image. By the time he went to Santiago in 1933 Parra considered himself a poet as well as a student of science, and he became a close associate of the literary and intellectual leaders at the student residence, the Internado Barros Arana, where he lived while he was studying for his degree at the Instituto Pedagógico. Carlos Pedraza and Jorge Millas were the acknowledged intellectuals at the residence, and gradually they introduced Parra to the significant ideas and figures of European and American culture, of which he was abysmally ignorant. He still laughs at the recollection of himself as the proverbial rustic who did not know what a Goethe was and had never heard

2. Leonidas Morales T., *La poesía de Nicanor Parra* (Santiago de Chile: Universidad Austral de Chile and Editorial Andrés Bello, 1972), p. 171. Subsequent references will be included in the text.

THE TRAJECTORY OF ANTIPOETRY 3

the names of Freud or Bergson. But by 1935 he had become acclimated to the heady atmosphere of avant-garde student intellectualism, which meant that he was esthetically and conceptually ready for the poetry he discovered in the *Antología de la poesía chilena nueva* (Anthology of New Chilean Poetry) that Eduardo Anguita and Volodia Teitelboim published in that year. The book was a revelation to Parra, who was especially enthusiastic about the humor and sense of playfulness, the literary experimentation and freedom which he found in the poetry of Vicente Huidobro [3] (Morales, p. 21). During the same year, Parra was also reading occasional pieces of surrealistic literature and writing poems for the shortlived student magazine *Revista nueva* (New Review) which he edited and published with Millas and Pedraza.

Of all the contemporary writers whose work Parra was discovering during this time of literary apprenticeship, the most important was Federico García Lorca. Parra's "Lorquian illumination" was the second decisive moment in the development of antipoetry. The *Romancero gitano* (Gypsy Ballads) was the model Parra systematically followed in the poems he composed in 1935-1936 and which he subsequently published as *Cancionero sin nombre* in 1937: "I had a

3. Vicente Huidobro (1898-1948) was the Chilean originator of Creacionismo (creationism), the avant-garde poetic movement of the years between the two World Wars, which insisted on the poet's obligation to create his own new reality rather than to imitate an already existing one.

Lorquian formation, and the most I could do was to introduce a few surrealistic images [into *Cancionero sin nombre*]. But even García Lorca used surrealism to some extent. In that anthology of Anguita's there was surrealism all over the place, surrealism *sui generis*, of course, but still perfectly acceptable" (Morales, p. 91). Parra now calls the volume an effort to "Chileanize García Lorca," but it received the Premio Municipal de Poesía in 1938, as well as enthusiastic praise from Gabriela Mistral: "We have before us a poet who will gain worldwide fame." [4] Other critics were scornful, however. Parra can still recite almost verbatim the devastating comments that appeared in Carlos Poblete's *Exposición de la poesía chilena* (Panorama of Chilean Poetry) (Buenos Aires: Editorial Claridad, 1941) p. 319: "He is the visible leader of a whole phalanx of 'guitar players' who have invaded a sector of Chilean poetry. It is poetry that is superficial, ephemeral, like everything else that is not the product of human reality." But what Poblete saw as shallow and trivial, one important commentator, the folklorist and poet Tomás Lago, viewed as a significant manifestation of the general movement toward a less obscure and more popular poetic style, and in 1938 he included Parra's works in the anthology of young poets which he

4. Margarita Aguirre and Juan Agustín Palazuelos, ed. and prol., *La cueca larga y otros poemas* by Nicanor Parra. (Buenos Aires: Editorial Universitaria, 1964), 5-14: p. 7. Subsequent references will be included in the text.

edited for the Sociedad de Escritores de Chile (Society of Chilean Writers). Eventually known as the Generation of 1938, these poets—Alberto Baeza, Hernán Cañas, Oscar Castro, Omar Cerda, Jorge Millas, Luis Oyarzún, Victoriano Vicario, as well as Parra—were profoundly affected by the Spanish Civil War both politically and poetically. As a consequence of their support of the Republican cause they became fervent admirers of the culture which seemed to best represent the beleaguered Spanish people. Furthermore, the Peninsular conflict stimulated a strong sense of community with those contemporary Spanish poets—Miguel Hernández, Rafael Alberti, Antonio Machado, and especially Federico García Lorca—who had used popular themes and forms in their writing. The natural concomitant of this sympathy among the young Chilean writers was their renewed interest in the enormous body of traditional Spanish folk ballads, the *romances*.[5]

Despite Parra's present day rejection of the poems from *Cancionero sin nombre* on the grounds that they are juvenilia, that they are not characteristic of his mature work and that he wrote the book during a period of "pure spontaneity" when he lacked a critical consciousness of the poetic art (Morales, p. 28), he admits that the conceptual, or theoretical, if not the formal origins of antipoetry can be found in the

5. Pablo García, "Contrafigura de Nicanor Parra," A, CXIX (1955), 150-163. Subsequent references will be included in the text.

shared attitude of the Generation of 1938 toward literature. They rejected the obscure, extravagantly metaphorical poetry of the earlier avant-garde, searching instead for a poetic idiom that would reflect popular and traditional speech rhythms. The tendency toward simplicity and the desire for accessibility were formalized and proclaimed publicly in 1942, when Tomás Lago edited *Tres poetas chilenos* (Three Chilean Poets) and wrote the prologue "Luz en la poesía (Light in Poetry) for this selection of poems by three members of the Generation: Castro, Vicario and Parra. Parra considers the anthology and Lago's esthetic formulations as a fundamental and significant documentation of his own developing theories about the poetic art: "Five years after the anthology of poets who were creationist, free-versist, hermetic, oneiric, priestly, we represented a kind of spontaneous, natural poetry which the mass public could understand ... Basically, I think we were correct in declaring ourselves the paladins of clear and natural means of expression. At least the great body of esthetic ideas in Chile have subsequently moved in that direction. In 1942 Tomás Lago ... became the commander-in-chief of the new doctrine whose content he himself summarized in the phrase 'Light in poetry.' ... The title of that preface was not arbitrary; just at that time Yours Truly had announced the publication of a book called 'La luz del día' (The Light of Day). The book never saw the light of day, but augmented and diminished, it later formed part of *Poemas y antipoemas.*[6]

Parra explains these modifications of diction and style, as well as his growing predilection for absolute transparency in his own work, as the outgrowth of a determination he made in the late 1930s that "poetry wasn't really working—there was a distance between poetry and life." Following the *Cancionero sin nombre* period of "pure spontaneity," his vision of poetry as a failed art had immediate consequences in his own literary consciousness. He decisively rejected the metaphorical, associative style of the older experimental poets (Neruda, Huidobro, the poets of the 1935 anthology) because it was "baroque, hermetic, cosmogonic," and he affirmed the need for a vernacular poetry dependent on ordinary life, expressive of common problems and accessible to the general public. Parra began his own kind of literary investigation, reading voraciously in an effort to locate the cause of what he considered poetry's failure to connect with the quotidian and the commonplace. His conclusion was that the "Renaissance esthetic" (which he defined as literature intended solely for the educated) lay at the root of contemporary poetic prob-

6. These remarks were first printed in *Atenea*, no. 380-381 (abril-septiembre 1958) and are cited in Fernando Alegría, "Nicanor Parra, el antipoeta," *CuA*, XIX, no. 3 (1960), pp. 209-220. Part of the statement also appears in Hugo Lindo, "Nicanor, antipoeta," *RepAm* (Mar. 1958), pp. 44-45.

lems, and he turned for a solution to "the marvels of the Middle Ages": not only the traditional Spanish ballads, but the poems of the Goliards, the troubadours, the Carmina Burana as well—writing that seemed spontaneous, vital and unmannered when compared to vanguardist poetry of the twentieth century. The conclusions he drew concerning the language of poetry—its uses and abuses—have remained essentially unchanged. Parra has rarely deviated from the theoretical course he set for himself after the publication of *Cancionero sin nombre,* and which can be stated as three closely allied directions or tendencies.

His first goal was to free poetry from the domination of the metaphor, "the abuse of earlier poetic language"; Parra views antipoetry as the definitive liberation from this "abusive" style since it consciously and consistently avoids special or "poetic" language in favor of direct communication with the reader. Second, he has insisted that antipoetry depend on the commonplace in all its ramifications, that it decisively reject the rarified and exotic, both thematically and linguistically. In 1939 he stated that "the language of literature must be no different from the language of the collectivity . . . language reflects the life of the people" (Skarmeta, p. 39), and in 1948 he proclaimed that the "function of the artist consists of rigorously expressing his personal experiences without any sort of commentary. To my mind the function of language is to be simply a vehicle, and I find the material that I work with in daily life ... and as for content, I'm also opposed to an exclusive romanticism. Anguish, despair, nostalgia are only some aspects of the human soul. Personally, I prefer to work with elements that are used less frequently: frustration and hysteria, the determining factors in modern life, are especially appealing to me" (García, p. 157). Third, Parra has reaffirmed the need to localize the language of antipoetry so that it would reflect a specific social reality. In 1939 he stated that his writing was leading directly to a "purely national expression" (Skarmeta, p. 39), and thirty-two years later he categorically insisted that "poetry can only be life in words—and life is in the commonplace. The poet is a common man. He is left in a vacuum when he removes himself from the community, the tribe—like what happens to a tree when it is removed from the earth: it withers, it dies." And he believes that the poet should use colloquialisms peculiar to his own country, even if readers from other areas find them difficult to understand.[7]

Parra's youthful rejection of the poets who had omitted "everyday problems" from their work seems to grow stronger with the passage of the years. For example, he calls Neruda a "singer" and claims that he prefers to speak: "Let the birds sing—man talks" (MF). And, to emphasize the vital relation between an

7. Parra made these remarks at a poetry reading held at New York University's Maison Française in May, 1970. Subsequent references to the reading will be included in the text as MF.

unlyrical, daily life and antipoetry, he has on occasion denied the existence of any literary roots at all for his poems. Despite all other statements to the contrary, he has insisted that antipoetry is an independent response to human circumstances rather than the fruit of a literary tradition (MF). Parra's negation of antecedents and influences is probably a whimsical exaggeration intended to confuse persistent academics, for he has repeatedly listed, in chronological order, the writers who have been important in his development (although he expresses his regret that he can be so easily influenced). In 1938, after his "Lorquian illumination" and the revelations of medieval literature, Parra began to explore Walt Whitman's poetry, using the Spanish translation of the Uruguayan poet Armando Vasseur (Morales, p. 192). Parra's response was overwhelming: "I discovered Whitman and freed myself from the poetry of García Lorca; Whitman was the solution to everything." He delighted in the unrestrained freedom of Whitman's language and subject matter: "It's an open poetry, there is no strict meter or conventional poetic language. The poems are like poetic studies, not little lyric verses. Description is very important in Whitman's poetry; there are even narratives, brief stories interpolated throughout his *Leaves of Grass* . . . the enormous quantity of materials and the freedom with which he works them, and a certain passionate vehemence with which he approaches certain themes, I think these were the lines of development in his poetry that touched me most deeply, so much so that I decided that all my previous work was out of focus, and I wrote no more little *romances* in the style of *Cancionero sin nombre*" (Morales, p. 192).

Most of what Parra wrote under the sway of Whitman's poetry was composed during the two years he spent in the United States. Between 1943 and 1945 Parra's mathematical studies at Brown University left him relatively little time for writing, but he did compose a group of twenty-one poems, "Ejercicios retóricos" (Rhetorical Exercises), which he now considers representative of a transitional stage between the Lorquian imitations of his first book and the mature antipoetry of his second. These poems, which were never published as a separate volume, did not appear in print until 1954, when they were included in the first issue of the magazine *Extremo Sur*. The unmistakable stylistic effects of this Whitmanesque period were Parra's experimentation with free verse and his use of a contemporary, urban background for his mournful hero;

> I am very alone and very anguished
> In front of a window at the hour of dusk,
> The gray New England sky,
> The vague memories of the distant homeland,
> The phantoms of solitude.
> . . . .
> . . . one can see a bridge and some empty
>   factories.
> The jam jars that accumulate in those places,
> The empty bottles,

The pages of old newspapers
Floating on dirty water . . .
(Morales, pp. 36-37)

Parra returned to Chile in 1946 and taught at the University for the next three years, a period that corresponds with the next phase in his recounting of influences on his poetry. He began to read the works of Franz Kafka, which convinced him that Whitman's universe—and his own writing as well—was deficient in that peculiar Kafkaesque sense of the comic. Parra yielded to Kafka's vision of the disastrously absurd in human affairs and fell easy prey to his "metaphysical laughter" (MF), to his ironic rendering of a tragically lunatic social and psychic order. "Kafka is a creator of atmospheres. That's important in my poetry too. My formulations are irrelevant in themselves. What gives them meaning is the allusion to a certain atmosphere. And there's another aspect of his work that is important in mine as well: the wavering between triviality and transcendence" (Skarmeta, p. 37).

Kafka's influence produced a full harvest of techniques, tonalities and perceptions which Parra individualized and incorporated into the antipoetic attitude and style. The consistent deformation both of reality and of the realistic, mimetic literary tradition—the subtle distortion of ordinary objects and phrases until they become the mire of sinister banality through which a helpless protagonist plods his torturous route to nowhere: Kafka's point of view was the absolute, diametrical opposite of Whitman's exuberant confrontation with the cosmos. And, Parra confesses, he could not maintain that heroic stance or that aggrandized vision of man: "Whitman's poems were Wagnerian poems, and I could occasionally fish those waters, but then . . . the characters began to fall apart and the hero was imperceptibly transformed into an antihero. At first this made me very uncomfortable, because I couldn't construct a heroic protagonist. . . . Only when I realized Whitman's limitations—something which I saw clearly through Kafka and other humorists, perhaps—only then did I realize the potential value . . . of a character who struggled to get into the poem, who was the antihero; all the rest, those Wagnerian chords, was out of focus. When I realized that the antihero had a perfect right to exist, then overnight I could write a poem like "La víbora" (The Viper). That was really the first of the post-Whitmanesque poems" (Morales, p. 193).

The bitterly comic nightmare of Kafka's world was in complete accord with the feel and technique of the surrealist literature that Parra was in the process of rediscovering during this period: "I was perfectly comfortable with the surrealist 'manifestoes' . . . I began to familiarize myself with this kind of literature. . . . It was on my return from the United States that I wrote 'La víbora,' 'La trampa' (The Trap) and 'Los vicios del mundo moderno' (The Vices of the Modern World)" (Morales, p. 194). These three poems, paradigms of antipoetic structure, tone and style, were published for the first time in 1948 when they appeared in the magazine *Pro-Arte* along with a critical study by Jorge Elliot (an Englishman living in Chile who was responsible for the first English translations of Parra's poems, and later collaborated with Lawrence Ferlinghetti for their publication in the City Lights Pocket Poet Series in 1960). They are written in Parra's mature style and clearly reflect the mutually complementary impact of Kafkaesque and surrealistic devices on antipoetry. Parra was not bound, in either poetic perception or execution, by a fixed realistic or esthetic convention, or by the Hispanic literary tradition. He had absorbed and made his own the principle of comic deformation: the delicate shift out of focus of the trivial details of an apparently absolute normality. The effect (not unlike that produced by what was later called "black humor") was an image of the quotidian world as lunatic, hostile or grotesque. The easy comfort of familiarity gave way to a queasy suspicion that the very density and predictability of that world had somehow gone awry with consequences that were more ludicrous than tragic:

Modern delinquents
Are authorized to meet daily in parks and
    gardens.
Provided with powerful binoculars and
    pocketwatches
They loot the kiosks favored by death
And install their laboratories among the
    flowering rosebushes. . . .

("Los vicios del mundo moderno")

The viper kept a detailed account book
Where she wrote down every penny I
    borrowed from her;
She didn't even let me use her toothbrush
    although I had given it to her myself
And she accused me of having ruined her
    youth;

(''La víbora'')

. . . for reasons that are hard to explain
I began to slide automatically down a kind of
    inclined plane,
Like a balloon losing air my soul lost altitude,
My instinct for self-preservation stopped
    working
And deprived of my most essential prejudices
I fell fatally into the trap of the telephone
That attracts everything around it, like an
    abyss.

(''La trampa'')

Parra was writing a kind of poetry that had not
been seen in Spanish before. Antiromantic, antirhe-
torical, antiheroic, antipoetic, he was ripe for his
"third and final illumination" which was to confirm
his position as the antipoet, stimulate the composition
of more poems in the developing new style and eventually lead to the publication of a book-length collection of poetry. The opportunity for revelation came in
the guise of a grant from the British Council to study

cosmology at Oxford University. Parra went to England in 1949, and for two years devoted more time to reading and writing poetry than to his scientific studies. He explored a wide range of traditional and contemporary English verse, but it was the effect of John Donne's "Holy Sonnet X," which he describes as a "trauma." The famous first lines—"Death be not proud, though some have called thee/Mighty and dreadful . . ."—had an enormous impact on Parra, and were the central, inspiring core of his English "illumination." He concluded rather arbitrarily that nothing like them had ever been written in his native language and that any poetry less powerful and expressive was "worthless." More than simply appreciative of Donne's genius, Parra was profoundly affected by it. The enduring effect of what began as enthusiastic admiration, but eventually became a radical rejection of one tradition and the simultaneous embracing of another, was to strengthen the tendencies already manifest in Parra's writing. He opened completely to the sympathetic influences of other English poets—W. H. Auden, C. Day Lewis, Stephen Spender and especially T. S. Eliot—where he found final confirmation of the antipoetic style. Eliot's radical transformation of poetic diction and his incorporation of prosaic phrases and colloquial language into his poems held a magnetic fascination for Parra, who translated some of the poetry he admired most into Spanish and committed lengthy portions of "The Waste Land" and the "Quartets" to memory. Eliot and the others had achieved something else as well: each had perfected the didactic possibilities of the idiomatic manner. They observed contemporary man and commented on his politics and manners, his religion and his society in the language of the modern city dweller. Their work gave sustenance to Parra's defiance of the "poetic" tradition in literature: "I had to get to England, even though I came to England after having written poems like 'La víbora,' 'La trampa,' 'Los vicios del mundo moderno' . . . I became fully conscious of the poet's craft in England . . . even those poems . . . were written in a period of relative unconsciousness" (Morales, p. 200).

The collection of poems which followed the English illumination was, of course, *Poemas y antipoemas.* Parra had considered other titles for the book, including "Oxford, 1950" and "Veinte años y un día" (Twenty Years and a Day: the crime of murder was punishable in Chile by that prison sentence), but he chose *Poemas y antipoemas* for "strategic reasons":[8] "I . . . noticed the book *Apoemas* by the French poet Henry Duche [in the window of a bookstore in Oxford]. So the word "antipoem" had already been used in the nineteenth century, though probably even the

8. His strategy was to capture the attention of the public with a title that was provocative and challenging. The most curious aspect of Parra's recounting of how he came upon the name for his book is that he has never mentioned Huidobro's use of the word in his well-known epitaph: "Here lies Vicente Huidobro, antipoet and wizard." Parra probably assumes that his readers take the connection for granted, for he has never forgotten his early debt to his Chilean predecessor: "Really, the master for me was Huidobro . . ." (Morales, p. 190).

18 THE ANTIPOETRY OF NICANOR PARRA

Greeks had used it. In any case the term came to me *a posteriori;* that is, I didn't write the book with a completely articulated theory in mind from the beginning" (Lerzundi, p. 65).

Poemas y antipoemas is divided into three sections, their differences documenting many of the transformations and modifications of antipoetry between 1938 and 1954. Parra characterizes Section I as "post-modernistic"[9] and "neo-romantic" (Morales, p. 199), full of "nostalgia with touches of irony." Consider, for example, these carefully hendecasyllabic lines from "Es olvido" (It is Forgetfulness):

I swear I don't even remember her name,
But I will die calling her Maria,
Not for a mere poet's whim:
Because she was like a provincial plaza.

On returning from school one afternoon
I learned of her undeserved death,

9. Postmodernism, usually dated 1910-1935, refers to the subdued, somewhat sentimental, often ironic style of the Latin American poets who reacted against the excesses and extravagances of Modernism, the major poetic movement of the late nineteenth and early twentieth centuries, comparable in many respects to the school of Parnasse in France, and originated by the Nicaraguan, Rubén Darío. Modernism had an enormous influence on the development of contemporary Latin American and Peninsular poetry, introducing new meters and reviving old ones, expanding and enriching the vocabulary, and using cosmopolitan and fairly exotic themes.

News that caused me such dismay
That I shed a tear when I heard it.
. . . .
Today is a blue spring day,
I think I will die of poetry
And of that famous melancholy girl.
I don't even remember her name.
I only know that she passed through this
    world
Like a fugitive dove:
I forgot her without wanting to, slowly,
Like everything else in life.

Parra calls Section II "expressionistic, with a certain
dissonance in the content." He describes the six works
as "twitching, nervous poems, there is a certain bru-
tality of expression in them, a bitterness, an acidity
and an aggressiveness . . ." (Morales, p. 199). "Auto-
rretrato" (self-portrait) exemplifies this sullen, mordant tone combined with meticulous rhyme and
meter:

Boys, consider
This mendicant friar's overcoat:
I am a teacher at an obscure high school,
I've lost my voice giving classes.
(After all or nothing
I do my forty hours a week)
. . . .
And all of it, for what?
To earn an unpardonable bread

As hard as a bourgeois' face
Smelling and tasting of blood.
. . . .
Nevertheless, I was once just like you,
Young, full of beautiful ideals,
I dreamed of founding copper
And polishing the facets of the diamond:
And here I am today
Behind this uncomfortable desk
Stupefied by the incessant ticking away
Of my five hundred hours a week.

It is Section III, however, that contains the writing which irreversibly affected the course of Latin American poetry. This portion of the book is composed of the "antipoems" in the title; Parra's catalogue of alleged influences on the genesis of the antipoems is wildly eclectic and could conceivably be expanded to include every serious humorist in the history of western civilization—or at least as many as Parra has knowledge of: "Here there's no more expressionism; they're a different kind of animal ... with all their debts to Kafka and surrealism. We should say too that they have to do with Chaplin's short films. ... While I was writing some of the most important antipoems, I was reading Kafka very carefully. But not only him: I also read the English poets. There are some critics who think *Poemas y antipoemas* comes directly out of English poetry. Well, it's a mixture of all that and many other things too.

The list is long and must include Aristophanes and Chaucer, for example" (Morales, pp. 199-200).

Perhaps as a result of the immediate and widespread recognition this volume received, Parra has brought his work to the public frequently and regularly since the appearance of *Poemas y antipoemas* in 1954. In contrast to the timidity he displayed after *Cancionero sin nombre*—he attributes the seventeen-year delay in publishing another book to critical attacks which he eventually accepted as valid—he has published three books of poems in Spanish *(La cueca larga* in 1958, *Versos de salón* in 1962 and *Canciones rusas* in 1967), two bilingual volumes *(Poems and Antipoems* in 1967 and *Emergency Poems* in 1972), his selected poems, *Obra gruesa*, in 1969, and his antibook postcard collection of the *artefactos* in 1972.

La cueca larga, at least superficially, appears to be a hearkening back to the folkloric orientation of *Cancionero sin nombre*. The two books employ a traditional and fixed popular form, and turns of phrase which recreate popular speech and humor. The four long poems which comprise this collection display a somewhat extravagant sense of humor and occasional surreal imagery in their representation of rustic diction, but they otherwise lie outside the main development of antipoetry:

I'm going to sing me a *cueca*
Longer than feeling

So my honey can see
That I'm nobody's fool

("La cueca larga" [The Long Cueca])

The most important of the three collections in
Spanish is *Versos de salón*.The antipoetic technique
crystalizes here, the poems are generally shorter than
those in *Poemas y antipoemas* and the sense of alienation is sharper, more acerbic and the humor more
pointed. In the eight years following *Poemas y antipoemas* Parra had taken firm hold of his public role
as antipoet and many of the most ironic poems are
really concentrated theoretical statements about
antipoetry:

For half a century
Poetry was
The paradise of the solemn fool.
Until I came along
And set up my roller coaster
Go on up if you like.
Of course I'm not responsible if you come
   down
Bleeding from your mouth and nose.

("La montaña rusa" [The Roller Coaster])

Versos de salón is also characterized by a metaphysical despair which contrasts significantly with the

circumscribed introverted suffering and frustration of the individual protagonist in *Poemas y antipoemas:*

Ladies and gentlemen:
I'm going to ask only one question:
Are we children of the sun or of the earth?
Because if we are only earth
I don't see why
We go on filming the picture:
I move the meeting be adjourned.

("Pido que se levante la sesión"
[I Move the Meeting Be Adjourned])

Parra believes that this collection represents a fully developed antipoetic technique which in *Poemas y antipoemas* was still in the process of maturation; the tonalities in *Versos de salón* are harder, perhaps more abrasive: "Starting with *Versos de salón* [antipoetry] is poetry written in the light of day, with a very brilliant outdoor atmosphere. The dark, gray atmospheres disappear. The images in *Versos de salón* are not in black and white: they are psychedelic colors, purple, chartreuse, yellow. That's the atmosphere, more or less, of *Versos de salón* and everything that comes afterwards, except *Canciones rusas*" (Morales, p. 201). Parra remarks a change in his poetic persona as well; he is transformed from a victimized antihero into a figure who is "odd," "extravagant," an "energumen" who hurls himself into hysterical confrontation with the world (Morales, pp. 215-216). And the structure of many poems corresponds to the frenzy of this protagonist, for there is a marked tendency toward a fragmented form that recalls a favorite device of the surrealists: chaotic enumeration and its suggestive juxtaposition of intentional *non sequiturs:*

Ham delivered to your door
Can you see time in a flower?
Secondhand crucifix for sale
Old age also has its reward
Funerals leave only debts:
Jupiter ejaculates on Leda
And the fuchsia looks like a ballerina.

("Versos sueltos" [Separate Verses])

Versos de salón provoked peculiarly virulent attacks from critics who hardly seemed able to contain their indignation. The most notorious and most frequently quoted of these was Father Salvatierra's: "In this work there is complete contempt for women, religion, virtue and beauty. I have been asked if this book is immoral. I would say no; it is too filthy to be immoral. A can of garbage is not immoral, no matter how many times we stir up its contents." Parra, as could be expected, treats such comments lightly, claiming that "no one is a poet in his own land" (Aguirre and Palazuelos, p. 7) and adding that "as soon as I showed my claws many people denied me" (Skarmeta, p. 57).

He has even incorporated Salvatierra's remarks into his poem "Test" ("La camisa de fuerza").

What is antipoetry:

. . . .
A container full of human excrement
As Father Salvatierra believes?

Rodríguez Monegal has called *Versos de salón* the end of the specifically antipoetic cycle in Parra's development as a writer,[10] but Parra contends that all his work is antipoetry "with modifications" and adds that he has never written antipoetry with the intention of having it conform to a fixed, consistent theory of composition. Parra calls his attitude "integralist," meaning that he is capable of a wide gamut of poetic responses and techniques, all of which are antipoetry. And indeed, his attitude toward stylistic variations in his writing is eminently pragmatic: he is the antipoet, and anything he writes is, by definition, antipoetry. Parra views his work as a vital extension of himself and therefore claims that antipoetry will continue to change as long as he lives. He has been obliged to engage in theoretical self-justifications like these because his critics have tended to formulate an antipoetic doctrine—on the basis of his past compositions—which admits to no deviation.

10. Emir Rodríguez Monegal, "Encuentros con Nicanor Parra," *MuN* no. 23 (mayo, 1968) pp. 75-83, p. 78. Subsequent references will be included in the text.

Such was the case with *Canciones rusas*, a collection of generally restrained, gentle poems which surprised and even disappointed those who had expected Parra to produce more controversial works in the style of *Versos de salón*. The book was written during his stay in the Soviet Union in 1963 and on his return to Chile in the following year. The poems first appeared in *Mundo nuevo*, no. 3 (Sept. 1966) and were published as a separate volume in 1967. Parra characterizes these poems as "postsymbolist . . . expressions of antipoetic lyricism." Although he has insisted that the root of his poetry is "truth" and not "beauty" and that the "search for beauty is an obstacle" for the poet, he justifies his frankly lyrical antipoems with a half-serious apology: "the lyric poets were to blame, not lyric poetry." The bittersweet flavor of most of *Canciones rusas* is an unusual emotion in the larger body of antipoetry, and the consistent tone of nostalgia and desolation prompted some commentators to accuse Parra of falling back into the rhetorical mire:

> Everytime I return
> To my country
>   after a long trip
> The first thing I do
> Is ask about those who have died:
> Every man is a hero
> For the simple fact of having died
> And heroes are our teachers.

And second
        about the wounded.

Only after
        not before complying with
This small funerary ritual
Do I consider myself entitled to live:
I close my eyes to see better
And rancorously sing
A turn-of-the-century song.

            ("Ritos" [Rituals])

But Parra did not altogether abandon the mordant
humor and the caustic appraisals of the ridiculous
that had earned him his reputation as the antipoet.
Surrounded by the elegiac melancholy of other works
in the collection, "Hace frío" ("It's Cold) is political
satire at its best:

We must be patient with the sun
He hasn't been seen anywhere
For forty days.

The Yankee astronomers
Examine the sky and frown
As if it were full of evil omens
And conclude that the sun is traveling
Through the underdeveloped countries
With suitcases full of dollars
On a mission of Christian charity.

And the Soviet scholars
—Who are about to send a man to the moon—
State that the sun
Is traveling through colonial empires
Photographing undernourished Indians
And mass executions of Blacks. . . .

Parra published his selected works in 1969. He used the title *Obra gruesa* (Basic Work: the title in Spanish suggests both a large, extensive work and the basic structure or skeleton of a building) and included only the poems that he considered essential to critical evaluations of his writing.[11] He omitted his earliest and most recent poems: *Cancionero sin nombre* because he thinks it is juvenilia, the *artefactos* (discussed below) because he deems them too controversial. *Obra gruesa* includes the complete *Poemas y antipoemas, La cueca larga, Versos de salón* and *Canciones rusas,* as well as three groups of poems which had not appeared as separate books, called "La camisa de fuerza", "Otros poemas" and "Tres poemas". Eleven poems from these collections had been published two years earlier under the title "Ejercicios respiratorios" in the bilingual edition of *Poems and Antipoems* (New York: New Directions, 1967).[12] These poems are, for the most part, free of the resigned,

11. Parra gave this information to Homero Aridjis in 1971; Mr. Aridjis very kindly shared notes of their conversation with me.

12. All of the "Ejercicios respiratorios" appeared in *Obra gruesa* as "Otros poemas" with the exception of "Acta de independencia" (Act of Independence), "Test," and "Padre nuestro" (Our Father), which were included under the title "La

wistful melancholy of *Canciones rusas*. They are
"pure" antipoems: laconic, comically bitter, sardonic,
often despairing, written in the barbed prosaisms
that galvanize the unsuspecting reader into a new
perception of overly familiar words and phrases:

camisa de fuerza." The poem "1930," listed as one of the *Poemas
y antipoemas* in the bilingual edition, is also included under the
title "Otros poemas."

Some of the poems show textual variations when one compares the version in the earlier bilingual edition with the version
in the selected works. These are listed below:

The poem "Jóvenes" (Young Poets: "Ejercicios respiratorios")
was incorporated in slightly altered form into "Cartas del poeta
que duerme en una silla" (Letters from the Poet Asleep in a
Chair: "Otros poemas"). The phrase "creo yo" (I think) was
added to line 5 in the *Obra gruesa* text, and the last two lines are
omitted.

The poem "Acta de independencia" in "La camisa de fuerza"
adds the final line "Plenamente consciente de mis actos" (Fully
conscious of my actions). In addition, the references to the poet's
age (forty-nine) and the year (1963) are two years earlier than
the poem in "Ejercicios respiratorios."

The poem "Test" in "La camisa de fuerza" omits line 25 of the
"Ejercicios respiratorios" version: "Una mujer con las piernas
abiertas" (A woman with her legs spread).

The poem "Padre nuestro" in "La camisa de fuerza" adds a
twelfth line: "No te preocupes de sus risas diabólicas" (Don't
worry about his diabolical laughter).

Emergency Poems (New York: New Directions, 1972), the
second bilingual edition of Parra's poems, includes all of "La
camisa de fuerza" except "Acta de independencia," "Padre
nuestro," "Test" and "Ultimas instrucciones" (Final Instruc-
tions) and these poems from "Otros poemas": "Juegos in-
fantiles" (Children's Games), "Jardín zoológico" (Zoological
Garden), "Sigmund Freud," "Manifiesto" (Manifesto), "Cartas
del poeta que duerme en una silla," "Telegramas" (Telegrams),
"Hombre" (Man) and "Los límites de Chile" (The Borders of
Chile).

. . . .
Our father who art where thou art
Surrounded by disloyal angels
Sincerely: don't suffer for us anymore
You have to realize
That gods are not infallible
And that we forgive everything.
          ("Padre nuestro" [Our Father])

Since 1967 Parra has composed hundreds of the
short, experimental poems which he calls *artefactos*
(artifacts). A few of them have appeared in
magazines, and in 1972 they were published as a collection of picture postcards illustrated by Guillermo
Teieda (Santiago: Universidad Católica de Chile,
1972). Parra's variable definitions of the *artefacto* are
unmistakably antipoetic in their diversity and
whimsical imprecision. In one of his most imaginative
descriptions of the controversial form (even his
friendliest critics hesitate concerning the extreme
reduction of discourse to minimal language in the
artefactos) Parra contends that they "resulted from
the explosion of the antipoem. They were so full of
pathos that they had to burst. The pieces are like the
fragments of a grenade. They go off in different directions and kill everyone in the area. They can be
thought of as 'elemental particles' . . . high velocity
and an enormous energy potential. They can easily
penetrate leaden walls, not because of their mass but
because of their speed . . ." (Skarmeta, p. 37). He has

also compared the *artefacto* to *haiku,* remarking on his interest in Zen and his "natural affinity" for Buddhism (MF). The similarity between the two forms is superficial at best. The traditional, classic form of the *haiku* is profoundly different from the free, found quality of Parra's compositions:

Cuba "sí,"
Yankees too.

("Simposio" [Symposium])

Humanities Students
Instead of writing filthy words
On bathroom walls
Write God
Write Holy Virgin

("Aviso" [Notice])

If I were president of Chile
I wouldn't leave a single puppet with his head
    intact,
I'd begin by declaring war on Bolivia
And then I'd put a bullet through my brain.

("Si yo fuera presidente de Chile"
            [If I Were President of Chile])

Parra has called the *artefactos* his effort to free Latin American poetry from "the plague of the hendeca-

syllable" although many of them employ a tradition-
ally accented eleven-syllable line, and one is even
titled "Endecasílabo" (Hendecasyllable):

Tell me if I annoy you with my tears

Despite Parra's "contradictory formulations" concerning these works, they appear to evolve naturally
and almost inevitably out of distinct tendencies in his
writing. The most significant of these is Parra's constant equation of spoken language to antipoetry.
They are (or should be) identical, and one of the antipoet's prime tasks is to recreate or reproduce slang,
jargon, clichés–the most familiar and frequent
threads in the fabric of ordinary language: "The poet
doesn't really create poetry, Parra was saying [in
1964]. He compiles it. The poet is an alert ear that
gathers poetry from the mouths of its speakers. This
spontaneous poetry only requires a minimal polishing
process, or a reordering of syllables, to convert it into
absolute poetry. Therefore, in the image suggested
by Parra, the poet travels through the world with his
ears open and a notebook near at hand, a notebook
that is filled with all the poetry that the collectivity
produces" (Rodríguez Monegal, p. 79). The antipoetic
function is to tape record in the field, to be "an
amoeba that feeds on everything that passes by."
Advertising slogans are perfect little poems (Morales,
p. 209):

Did you McLean your teeth today?

and the dry, uninspired language of statistics can be shifted only slightly to produce one of the most poignant and compelling of the *artefactos:*

One out of every thousand Chileans
dies of sorrow.

Parra has elaborated this theory of the poet as selector, rather than creator, of his poems, and has rather dogmatically defined the poetic function as one of choosing "those spoken texts which are most intense, most significant, the ones that contain the greatest amount of energy and can stand up by themselves. In practical terms the poet's work might well become like the entymologist's, who goes out hunting insects.... Literary expression has been replaced by spoken expression, and it seems that what poets as well as prose writers are looking for today is the cultural spirit of each country in what you might call the genius of the language. That's the right road. We're no longer interested in literature for literature's sake, but in literature for man's sake: we're looking for ourselves, if that phrase means anything, and it seems that one possible way is through the spoken word, and that on any other track we don't get anywhere ... poetry has to do with human experience in its entirety, with the totality of man, and the fact is that literature should also have its little corner somewhere in the speech of the poet.... It can't be discarded because, to paraphrase, nothing human can be alien to the poet" (Morales, pp. 206-208).

The *artefactos* compress, delineate and formalize the fragmented quality which, with *Versos de salón*, had become increasingly important in antipoetry. In this sense the *artefactos* are the product of Parra's ingenious handling of the chaotic enumeration technique. He has carried the device to its extreme although logical conclusion: each line becomes an independent entity rather than a component element in a grouping of phrases which are bound together by the free associations of automatic writing. For example, each statement in a poem like "Frases" (Sentences—"La Camisa de fuerza") could, once the antipoem has "exploded," be an *artefacto:*

Let's not kid ourselves
The automobile is a wheelchair
The lion is made of sheep
Poets have no biography
Death is a collective habit
Children are born to be happy
Reality tends to disappear
Fornication is a diabolical act
God is a good friend of the poor.

These lines are *artefactos* before the fact; they have been forced into a semblance of coherence under a single title (an act of antipoetic prowess with a specific comic intention—to satirize the surrealist assumption that disparities are unified because they emerge from an individual unconscious mind). From another point of view, Parra needed only to separate what had been awkwardly joined together in order to create an *artefacto*.

Finally, the very term "artifact" suggests an anthropological document. In this sense Parra comes back to his view of the poet-as-tape recorder in the *artefactos*. Here, for posterity, he records in its most spontaneous form the kind of language by which contemporary man lives—the hard, material, linguistic fact of his daily existence, which may encompass either trivia or the most piercing despair:

You never tell me the truth.   **1951194**

(untitled)

Either God is everywhere
or He's absolutely nowhere

("Ultimátum")

Say openly that she killed herself
She committed suicide with a bullet through
    her brain

("Hay cortesías que merecen palos"
                [There are Courtesies that
                Make You Want to Kill])

Parra's ripening sense of devotion to the mass speaker of Spanish as his prime source of antipoetry (ultimately manifested in his writing as the *arte-*

facto) may well be causally related to his explicit political involvements of the early 1960s. He calls this period a time of "minimal distance between antipoetry and politics," and that proximity is expressed in its most partisan form in the volume *Discursos* (Speeches) (Santiago: Nascimento, 1962). The first half of the book contains what Parra now calls his "antipoetic prose": the speech of welcome to Pablo Neruda when he was made an honorary member of the Facultad de Filosofía y Educación (School of Philosophy and Education) at the University; Neruda's acceptance speech on the same occasion comprises the second half of the volume. In this formal, public statement Parra makes a *sui generis* defense of strict social radicalism in literature which, in a certain sense, is a simple recasting in doctrinaire terms of those same ideas about poetry which he had nurtured throughout his literary career. His enthusiasm for what he calls Neruda's expansion of the traditional poet's egoistic self into a public, communal "we" [13] is, except for the set, dogmatic phrases, not unlike his own vision of the antipoet as society's historiographer whose art springs, almost full-blown, from the mouth of the masses: "The mission successfully carried out by Pablo Neruda during his forty years of spiritual investigation has been to suppress false individual problems that artificially obscure

13. Pablo Neruda and Nicanor Parra, *Discursos* (Santiago de Chile: Nascimento, 1962), p. 31. Subsequent references will be included in the text.

one's vision, and to propose, and immediately offer the appropriate solution to, real problems. It would seem that from this there emerges the lesson that the *plenitude* of the individual is the natural result of his proper integration into the *social struggle*. Outside of that, outside the social struggle, all is sorrow, all is darkness, all roads lead to madness. Contemporary man can very well drug himself with whisky, with religion, with pure art, with sex, with words, with gold, with blood, with any of the poisoned fruits of bourgeois culture, but he cannot feel well, he cannot breathe deeply, he cannot blossom in all the splendor of his body and his spirit except by fulfilling his obligations as contemporary man" *(Discursos,* pp. 44-45).

One of these "obligations" for the antipoet is to "integrate the human race—to speak in the name of the species." In theory at least, his work has value because of the anonymous community that unconsciously creates it. Although the legendary "Folk" is a supremely romantic invention, it served as a convenient theoretical foil for the opposition which Parra established between the "collectivity" and an equally romantic conception of the artist as essentially different from and superior to the common mass of men. The cult of the creative individual was, for Parra, during his politicizing period, not only bourgeois but "poetic." "Manifiesto," one of the most carefully objective and humorless poems ever written by Parra (it is discussed at greater length in Chapter 2) reaffirms the value of antipoetry as an art form which is "properly integrated into the social struggle." The poem is a restatement of many points that Parra touched on in his speech, now applied directly to his own writing.

> Ladies and gentlemen
> This is our final word,
> —Our first and final word—
> The poets have come down from Olympus.
> . . . .
> Unlike our elders
> —And I say this with all due respect—
> We maintain
> That the poet is not an alchemist
> The poet is a man like everyone else
> A mason who builds his wall:
> A builder of doors and windows.
>
> . . . .
> But their poetry was a disaster
> Second hand surrealism
> Third hand decadence
> Old wood washed up by the sea.
> Adjective poetry
> Nasal and guttural poetry
> Arbitrary poetry
> Poetry copied out of books
> Poetry based
> On the revolution of the word
> . . . ."
> When in fact it should spring
> From a revolution of ideas.

. . . .
Instead of poetry in the clouds
We offer
Poetry on solid ground
—Cold head, warm heart
We are committed to the solid ground—
Instead of café poetry
The poetry of nature

Instead of salon poetry
The poetry of the public square
The poetry of social protest.

"Manifiesto" clearly takes its esthetic cues from
rigidly circumscribed definitions of "revolutionary"
and "bourgeois," and Parra succumbs to the easy
temptation of using these terms as positive and
negative judgments of literary value. But the
evidence of his other antipoems indicates that his
apparently doctrinaire commitments were more a
temporary extension of Parra's antiestablishment
position as a writer than the reflection of an orthodox
political ideology. Parra has composed few poems of
"social protest" in any strict dogmatic sense of the
phrase. Even so militant a work as "Sigmund Freud,"
written after his trip to the People's Republic of
China in 1963, is more than balanced by other poems
which indicate his rejection of singleminded political
points of view. In "Sigmund Freud," then, Parra
derides psychiatry as the emblematic cornerstone of a
decadent capitalist culture while he extols the virtues
of the new Chinese society:

It's in the works of Freud where one finds
The wildest statements.
· ·
We see a god nailed to a cross
A crucifix is a phallic symbol
We buy a map of Argentina
To study the border problem
All of Argentina is a phallic symbol
They invite us to People's China
Mao Tse Tung is a phallic symbol
· ·
In the airport at Peking
It's hotter than all of hell
They're waiting for us with flowers and cold
    drinks.
Not since I've had the use of my reason
Have I seen such beautiful flowers.
Not since the world has been a world
Have I seen such pleasant people
Not since the planets have been planets
Have I seen such happy people

Not since I was thrown
Out of the Garden of Eden
· ·

The West is a huge pyramid
That ends and begins with a psychiatrist:
The pyramid is about to crumble.

But only a few years later his disillusionment with the

politics (or politicians) of the left, and his simultaneous return to the ironic, antipoetic view of man's
affairs, were expressed in this poem:

IF THE POPE DOESN'T BREAK WITH THE USA

if the Kremlin doesn't break with the USA
if Luxembourg doesn't break with the USA
why the hell should I

would someone please tell me
why the hell should Iiiii . . . !

("Si el Papa no rompe con el USA"
[If the Pope Doesn't Break with the USA])

and in the angry—and comic—acrostic *artefacto*, in
which the first letter of each line spells the Spanish
equivalent of "crap," and the six lines translate as
"Leftist Movement of Revolutionary Writers of
America:

Movimiento
Izquierdista
Escritores
Revolucionarios
De
América

In his present day disclaimer of "Manifiesto" (and by
extension "Sigmund Freud"), Parra states categor-

ically that "the antipoet is not a preacher ... I'm suspicious of the philosopher's stone—of doctrines" and insists that the poem "is not the manifesto of antipoetry but the product of a specific and personal moment." What he is clearly denying are the radical politics of the "social struggle" taken as a matter of inherent interest to the poet or as the sole valid means of judging his work. He is still adamantly scornful of the use of poetry as a vehicle for "self-expression" when the self expressed is unduly exalted or takes refuge in the obscurity of elitism; he is still the absolute antiromantic: "antipoetry is a collection of masks in which 'I' does not exist."

Parra's most recent published poetry is only peripherally political, but he has maintained and renewed his dry, comic vision of the world and its vagaries, disappointments and frustrations. The social condition can be as grotesque and absurd as the human one—and as acidly laughable—when they are viewed through the crooked but sharply focused lens of antipoetry:

I JEHOVAH DECREE

the end of everything once and for all
I'm finished with the solar system

we must return to the maternal womb
I wash my hands of the whole affair

let no one escape
let everything end at once
what's the point in beating around the bush

the War in Viet Nam is just fine
prostate operations are just fine
I Jehovah decree old age

all of you make me laugh
all of you get on my nerves
only a born imbecile
kneels down to worship a statue

frankly I don't know what to say to you
we're on the brink of the Third World War
and nobody seems to notice anything

if you destroy the world
do you think I'm going to create it again?

("Yo Jehová decreto" [I Jehovah Decree]

CHAPTER II

The Theory
of Antipoetry

Parra dearly loves the role of manifesto-maker; he consciously and actively enjoys goading the bourgeoisie, wherever and whenever he can. Consequently, one must be on guard when searching for clear information about his poetic theories in formal interviews, for Parra often treats them as "anti-interviews." His responses vary according to the question and the questioner, and can even be intentionally misleading and inconsistent. The task of defining his poetic precepts is not hopeless, however. Parra has written many poems which are actually theoretical statements concerning his work, his literary function as the antipoet, and the problem of how and why poetry should be written. Specifically, they deal with the nature of antipoetry: how it differs from poetry,

45

its effect on the reader, its place in contemporary society.

The poems about poetry are basically reliable evidence for a formulation of Parra's program for literary renovation and poetic change. In them he predictably adheres to his most important esthetic dictum—"real seriousness is comic"—which he expounds in a poem included in the *Discursos*, pp. 14-16:

Seriousness with a frowning brow
(We read in one of the antipoems)
Is an old maid's seriousness
Seriousness with a frowning brow
Is a literary expert's seriousness
Seriousness with a frowning brow
Is a parish priest's seriousness
Real seriousness is different:
The seriousness of Kafka
The seriousness of Charlie Chaplin
The seriousness of Chekhov
The seriousness of Quijote's author
The seriousness of the man with the glasses [1]
(Once there was a man attached to a nose,
It was a superlative nose)

1. The "man with the glasses" is Francisco de Quevedo (1580-1645), one of the great writers of the Spanish baroque. He is known as a satirist and a moralist, in both poetry and prose, and was the author of one of the most famous of the picaresque novels, *El Buscón*. The lines in parentheses are taken from his satirical, comic poem, "A una nariz" (To a Nose).

The seriousness of the Catholic Church
The seriousness of the Armed Forces
(Once there was a man attached to a nose
It was a superlative nose)
The seriousness of the Hydrogen Bomb
The seriousness of President Kennedy
Are a cemetery-keeper's seriousness
Real seriousness is comic.

The poem, in its technique as well as in its defense of humor as an expressive medium, is a paradigmatic example of antipoetry. Its theme is developed in colloquial language, with a parenthetical parody of academic solemnity. The apparent lightheartedness, the familiar lines from Quevedo, the unadorned cataloguing of the various kinds of seriousness and the repetition of the word "seriousness" in a series of syntactically identical sentences, all lull the reader into a state of somnolent nonexpectancy, rudely disturbed when he realizes that he has read a pointed social diatribe and a very precise statement of antipoetic theory. Parra succeeds in preaching at the reader and "galvanizing" him, but avoids the appearance of an insufferable didacticism. The three theoretical poems which are studied in this chapter employ very much the same devices. "Advertencia al lector" (Warning to the Reader), "Cambios de nombre" (Name Changes) and "Manifiesto" (Manifesto) are explicit and for the most part comic statements of Parra's poetic theory, and excellent examples of the practice of antipoetry. His notion of why and how he writes is developed in these poems on poetry. The ideas he expresses can illuminate any investigation of what antipoetry is and help define the artistic commitments which are its source.

"Advertencia al lector" is the first poem in Section III of *Poemas y antipoemas,* and the sixteen poems of this section of the book are the first important group of antipoetic works published by Parra. As the title suggests, "Advertencia al lector" is an introduction and a warning that the antipoems of Section III are not what the reader might expect after the poems he has read in the first two sections.

> The author will not answer for the annoyances
>   which his writings may cause:
> Although it pains him
> The reader will always have to think of
>   himself as satisfied.
> Sabellius, who besides being a theologian was
>   a consummate humorist,
> After having reduced the dogma of the Holy
>   Trinity to a pile of dust
> Did he perhaps answer for his heresy?
> And if he did answer, how did he do it?
> In what a mad way!
> Basing his answer on such a mountain of
>   contradictions!

According to the doctors of the law this book
   should not have been published:
The word rainbow does not appear anywhere
   in it
Much less the word sorrow,
The word torquate.
But there are plenty of chairs and tables,
Coffins! desk accessories!
Which fills me with pride
Because, in my opinion, the sky is falling.

Mortals who have read Wittgenstein's
   Tractatus
Can really blow their own horns
Because it is a difficult work to get hold of:
But the Vienna Circle was dissolved years
   ago,
Its members have dispersed without leaving
   a trace
And I have decided to declare war on the
   cavalieri della luna.

My poetry may very well lead nowhere:
"The laughter in this book is false!" my
   detractors will argue
"Its tears, artificial!"
"Instead of sighing on these pages, one
   yawns"
"He stamps his feet like an infant"

"The author expresses himself by means of
  sneezes"
Agreed: I invite you to burn your ships,
Like the Phoenicians I am trying to make my
  own alphabet.

"Why bother the public then?" my friendly
  readers will ask themselves:
"If the author himself begins by criticizing
  his writings,
What can we expect from them?"
Watch out, I'm not criticizing anything
Or, better yet, I'm exalting my point of view,
I'm proud of my limitations
I'm praising my creations to the skies.

Aristophanes' birds
Buried the corpses of their fathers
In their own heads.
(Every bird was really a flying cemetery)
In my opinion
The time has come to modernize this
  ceremony
And I will bury my plumes in the heads of
  my friendly readers!

Parra begins the poem with a sly disclaimer of
responsibility for the unpleasant effects of antipoetry
on the unsuspecting reader. His sardonic apology
for these "annoyances" sets the tone of parodic self-criticism which he develops throughout the

rest of the work.[2] He goes on to equate antipoetry with the writing of Sabellius, Wittgenstein and Aristophanes in a series of implicit comparisons which center on the crucial matter of clarity in both thought and language. Alternating with the historical references, and simultaneously growing out of them as a result of the understood comparisons, are Parra's critical statements regarding the differences between poetic and antipoetic language. Again the emphasis is on clarity and accessibility as Parra stresses the distinct vocabularies and attitudes of poetry and antipoetry and elucidates for the reader in manifesto fashion what the antipoet avoids and what he favors in the spheres of language and emotional expressiveness. But the broad theory of antipoetry is formulated most succintly in the historical examples of men with whom Parra feels a strong literary and philosophical connection.

The first is Sabellius, associated with the effort early in the history of the Church to clarify and simplify the logical and theological complexities inherent in the doctrine of the Trinity. Sabellius lived in the first half of the third century, and was an important member of the movement, originated by Noetus, which insisted that God was ultimately indivisible.

2. The theme of the poet's not being responsible also appears, in varying contexts, in "La montaña rusa" (The Roller Coaster), "Se me pegó la lengua al paladar" (My Tongue has Stuck to my Palate), "Viva la cordillera de los Andes" (Long Live the Andes Mountains), "Discurso fúnebre" (Funeral Oration), "Yo pecador" (I, a Sinner), "Ponchartrain Causeway", and "Me retracto de todo lo dicho" (I Take Back Everything I've Said).

This school of thought, engaged in a defense of strict monotheism, maintained that the designations "Father," "Son" and "Spirit" (or Creator, Redeemer and Life of the Church) were actually descriptions of different phases or aspects of the Godhead rather than definitions of separate and distinct entities.[3]

The effort to abandon obscurity is the basis for Parra's association of his work with Sabellius's. The antipoet finds himself embarked on a comparable simplifying—and therefore "heretical"—enterprise. In Parra's terms clarity, simplicity and intellectual accessibility are the heresies against orthodoxy in literature as well as theology. In an unprepared or hostile public such iconoclasm provokes the kind of reaction that Parra makes use of in his ironic treatment of Sabellius. When he alludes to Sabellius's responses to his detractors as mad or contradictory he is assuming the orthodox and critical point of view of the offended traditionalists and at the same time identifying himself with Sabellius. These phrases actually anticipate negative criticisms of antipoetry and, very subtly, Parra's sardonic treatment of them makes the criticisms untenable.

The second reference is to Wittgenstein and the Vienna Circle. Their major effort in philosophy was to strip language bare of metaphysical complexities, to clarify it and make it an efficient tool of philosophical

3. See James Hastings, ed., *Encyclopedia of Religion and Ethics* (New York: Charles Scribner's Sons, n.d.), vols. I, VII, VIII and Frank Thilly, *A History of Philosophy*, rev. Ledger Wood (New York: Henry Holt & Co., 1951), pp. 170 ff.

investigation. Beginning with the fundamental proposition that philosophy must study thought and ideas through the intermediary of language, Wittgenstein made a thorough analysis of the limits of language—that is, what in fact it is possible to say sensibly—and attempted to clarify the difference between sense and nonsense in factual discourse. His books, especially *Philosophical Investigations*, have been described as "a new kind of philosophical work which contains no sweeping generalization and remarkably little categorical assertion ... full of perfectly ordinary detailed descriptions of language, which are presented dialectically in a way that invites the reader to take part in the dialogue." [4]

Two factors are of special interest in relating Wittgenstein's philosophy of language to antipoetry. The first is the dependence on the reader for the success of the method. Parra invites the reader's participation in all of the theoretical poems (Chapter 3 will discuss at length the ironic structure of the antipoems that often requires the perceptions of the reader for its completion). Second, there is the radical change in philosophical method which Wittgenstein effected. Parra finds this comparable to his own efforts to clear away metaphorical and obscure language from poetry. Significantly, he calls Wittgenstein the "anti-philosopher," and speaks of his meeting with the philosopher, during his stay in

4. David Pears, *Ludwig Wittgenstein* (New York: Viking Press, 1970), p. 5.

England, with a strong sense of kinship and admiration.

For the theoretical purposes of this poem, Parra's view of the function and nature of antipoetry is supported by the work of Sabellius and Wittgenstein, whose philosophical and linguistic concerns are similar to his. The antipoet too is engaged in a struggle—almost mortal combat—to strip language of its metaphorical and metaphysical accretions, to simplify its vocabulary and make it an efficient tool of investigation and literary expression, in short, to transform poetry into antipoetry. Parra emphasizes his preoccupation with normalizing the language of poetry in the semiserious list of words that he boasts of having eliminated from his writing. He has replaced "rainbow," "sorrow" and "torquate" with "chairs and tables," "coffins," and "desk accessories." He has substituted the inescapable material data of ordinary life for the lyric sentimentality and exoticism of the romantic tradition in poetry. He has created antipoetry because he feels morally obliged to investigate, analyze and clearly express the sometimes terrible, often banal *why, what* and *how* of the physical world he inhabits, and to communicate his insights directly to the reader. In the shared analytic and clarifying impulse, and in the denigration of a tradition presented as nonsensical, inadequate and irrelevant, Wittgenstein is one of Parra's spiritual ancestors, if not a direct source for his experimentation

Humor lies at the core of antipoetry, and the

somber, somewhat pompous tones of this line of rea-
soning require some comic lightening. Parra consistently tempers his serious theoretical statements
with prosaic, derisive or comic elements. For example,
he interjects the prosaic phrase "in my opinion" immediately after his exposition of a program for linguistic renovation, which is followed in turn by an
allusion to the end of the world in the language of
Chicken Little ("the sky is falling"). The effect is
deflationary and self-critical. It provokes a mocking
response in the reader when Parra himself under-
mines his own pomposity and sabotages his own
overblown dignity. Yet he clearly means to be taken
seriously as an innovator despite the brusque nonsense—the comic relief—that he employs as a diver-
sionary tactic. He makes an open declaration of war
on the "cavalieri della luna," defined by Parra as the
"Juan Ramón Jiménez kind of poet."[5] Since Wittgenstein has died and the Vienna Circle has dispersed, these comrades-in-arms—and Sabellius as
well—can no longer do battle with the mystifying
obscurantists and academicians, who are equivalent
in this context to the poets who view the material of
their art as different from and superior to the spoken

5. Parra made this observation to Professor Alexander
Coleman of New York University, who very kindly shared the
notes of their conversation with me. Juan Ramón Jiménez
(1881-1958), the Nobel-Prize-winning Spanish poet, exemplifies
literary devotion to the search for absolute beauty, ineffability,
lyricism and musicality in poetry. He was an important expo-
nent of the symbolist-modernist tradition in Hispanic poetry.

language. Parra the heretic, the humorist, the proponent of simple speech and the committed enemy of metaphysics and metaphors sees himself as their descendant and natural successor in the struggle against the "cavalieri della luna" and the "doctors of the law" who are unable or unwilling to clarify, simplify and analyze reality, unable or unwilling to make anyone laugh or to laugh at their own self-importance, unable or unwilling, in short, to compose poetry that Parra deems worth preserving. The obvious exaggerations of his case prepare the reader for the sharp distinctions between poetry and antipoetry which follow in the fourth and fifth stanzas.

Parra interrupts the series of historical examples and returns to the subject of his own work. He elucidates the "annoyances" (alluded to at the beginning of the poem) that antipoetry may cause the reader, and uses this same material to mount an apparent attack on antipoetry. His technique is to assume the voice of his detractors and then to respond to them as the antipoet. The responses are ambiguous and ironic, for he agrees with his presumptive critics that antipoetry suffers from all the defects they attribute to it, but he simultaneously insists that these flaws are precisely what distinguish his work from the poetry of the "cavalieri della luna." The alleged defects of antipoetry are actually its virtues. Parra lists them in a careful order which, *mutatis mutandi*, develops into a strongly worded defense of antipoetry.

First, his work is charged with being inconclusive

("My poetry may very well lead nowhere"). Parra suggests a contrast with the fixed conclusions, fixed forms and predictable emotions that inimical poetry might provide. Recalling his ironic criticism of Sabellius in the first stanza, Parra seems to imply that the alleged inconclusiveness of antipoetry is in fact an unorthodox, antidoctrinal position which the theologian and the antipoet share. Then, he is attacked for having abrogated hyper-romantic, melodramatic emotionalism in his poetry ("The laughter in this book is false, . . ./Its tears, artificial"). Because it does not engage in or appeal to sentimentality, antipoetry may very well bore the unprepared reader ("Instead of sighing, on these pages one yawns"). Parra depicts his audience as shallow and sentimental, as the "friendly readers" whose notion of poetic expressiveness is limited by their own easy emotionalism. Parra sardonically pretends to be solicitous for their sensibilities, and consequently makes certain that we identify ourselves as a more sophisticated audience who can only feel scornful amusement and superiority toward the one addressed in the poem. The antipoet is also accused of petulance, of expressing himself by means of temper tantrums ("He stamps his feet like an infant"). Parra's most profound feelings and responses do not take the orthodox "poetic" form that the limited reader has come to expect. Parra's language is not noble, his despair is not exemplary, his tone is neither amiable or philosophical. Finally, the worst—or best—of the accusations is that Parra's writing is devoid of lyr-

icism ("The author expresses himself by means of
sneezes"). There is no music in his work; the sounds of
his poetry are as harsh and as abrupt as an eruptive
sneeze. Antipoetry does not soothe the reader, or
convince him, or exalt him. It rudely disturbs him.

The antipoet agrees—ironically. All of the "annoyances" of which he is accused are true, but if the
reader wishes to join Parra in his experiment, in his
adventurous search for a new mode of poetic expression, then he must abandon these objections. They
amount to no more than a nostalgic defense of a
tradition which is presented as worn out, incom-
prehensible and steeped in a banal emotionalism that
does no service to the feelings it ostensibly expresses.
Parra does not question the validity of the emotions
in traditional poetry. He objects to the language in
which they are expressed.

The reader, therefore, should join with the antipoet
who, like Cortés, will burn the fleet to insure the
loyalty of those too cowardly to explore *terra incog-
nita* voluntarily ("... I invite you to burn your ships").
Parra abruptly changes the frame of reference, but
not the intention of this section of the poem, by
stressing the dangerous originality of his literary
adventure. He states that like the Phoenicians he is
creating a new alphabet, that is, a new vocabulary and
language for poetry which are as crucial to the
development of communication as the achievement of
the Phoenicians. Parra glories in the creative risks of
the enterprise but again pulls back from the exalted
vision, or rather, from the hyperbolic propagandizing

of his pronouncements. He achieves the necessary comic distance from his exaggerated position by establishing a sense of disparity or incongruity between the statements he is making and the language he uses for making them. The banality of prosaic words and phrases like "watch out" and "point of view" seems to subvert his affirmations of the value and originality of antipoetry. The contrast between his absolutely serious self-defense and the intentionally humorous and arrogant comparison of his efforts and accomplishments to those of Cortés and the Phoenicians has the same effect. Parra is attempting to disorient the reader and irritate his tenderest poetic sensibilities. In a very real sense the reader's eventual acceptance of the linguistic incongruities of antipoetry—indeed, the incongruities themselves—are the adventure Parra glorifies in this poem, and in which he invites the reader to participate.

Parra returns to the historical examples, referring to Aristophanes with a paraphrase of a passage from *The Birds:*

Aristophanes' birds
Buried the corpses of their fathers
In their own heads.

In the play the lark is described as the first creature, born even before Earth. Since Earth did not yet exist, the bird had no place to bury his father when he died and finally, in desperation, he entombed him in his own head. The playwright capable of creating sheer comedy like this may well be the most important of the historical figures listed in "Advertencia al lector." Parra has called him the "anti-Aristotelian spirit" among the ancient Greek writers because he did not conform to what Parra considers the essence of Greek culture—"the hymn to beauty, not life." Aristophanes embodies those elements of burlesque and satire which are the only literary tradition that the antipoet wholeheartedly accepts as his own. Parra refers to him frequently when he discusses the authors who have influenced antipoetry, and he devotes the first section of the poem "Total cero" (Complete Zero) to Aristophanes:

> Death doesn't even respect genuine humorists
> as far as she's concerned all jokes are bad ones
> even though it's she personally
> who teaches us the art of laughing
> let's take the case of Aristophanes
> kneeling right down on his knees
> laughing like a madman right in the face of
> Fate:
> if it had been up to me I would have saved
> such a precious life
> but if Death doesn't respect John Doe
> why should she respect Thomas Toe, Richard Roe
> or Harry Hoe?

Aristophanes is a model of comic relevance for Parra, and the antipoet calls attention to both aspects of his

art in this poem.[6] He was one of the first serious
humorists in European literature, his comedy had
critical, satirical and political purposes, and his
talents lay in just those areas which appeal most to
Parra's perception of his own literary role. It is fitting
that the reference to *The Birds* leads directly into the
half-serious threat that concludes the poem: "And I
will bury my plumes in the heads of my friendly
readers." The antipoet, as literary counterpart of the
first creature, will bury his dead (the "cavalieri della
luna") in the heads of his reluctant "friendly
readers." "Plumes" is equivalent both to corpses
(through the association of plumes and birds) and to
poetry and poets (through the association of plumes,
pens and writing). The parodic final warning is really
Parra's ultimate challenge to the reader to join with
him in burying the past and exploring the antipoetic
New World. Both readers and antipoet are the children of the same poetic orthodoxy. The creation of
antipoetry and the conscious negation of the lyrical
and sentimental tradition in poetry, the search for a
new mode of expression and the affirmation of our
legitimate spiritual ancestry—Aristophanes, Sabel-

6. In the play *The Babylonians* Aristophanes satirized the
politics and policies of the empire. The attack provoked Cleon to
prosecute him for treason. In a subsequent play, *The Achar-
nians*, Aristophanes referred to the incident stating that he
"had such a rolling in the dirt as all but killed him." Gilbert
Murray, *The Literature of Ancient Greece*, 3rd ed. (Chicago:
University of Chicago Press, 1956) p. 281.

lius, Wittgenstein—should be a mutual task, although Parra suspects that his "friendly readers" may be unwilling partners to the enterprise.

In "Cambios de nombre" Parra establishes a feeling of hostile distance between himself and his public. The readers are his enemy, and he seems to rescind the invitation proffered in "Advertencia al lector." The poem is the first work in *Versos de salón*, a volume which Parra considers one of his most important collections of antipoems, and like "Advertencia al lector," "Cambios de nombre" warns the reader of what is to follow:

> To the lovers of belles-lettres
> I send my very best wishes
> I am going to change the names of some
>   things.
>
> My position is this:
> The poet isn't keeping his word
> If he doesn't change the names of things.
>
> Why should the sun
> Keep on being called the sun?
> I ask that it be called Pussycat,
> The one with the forty-league boots!
>
> My shoes look like coffins?
> Be it known that from this day on
> Shoes are called coffins.

Spread the news, make a note, publish the
  fact
That shoes have changed their name:
From now on they are called coffins.

All right, it's been a long night
Every poet with any self respect
Should have his own dictionary
And before I forget
We have to change the name of god himself
Let everyone call him whatever he wants:
That's a personal problem.

In this poem Parra claims complete artistic independence from both his critics and his readers, and warns
that he will effect drastic alterations in the vocabulary
of poetry, in the language itself. He intends to destroy the old idiom, a necessary prelude to the
profoundly new poetic language that he is in the
process of creating in the antipoems. Destruction and
creation of the means of communication are the re-
sponsibilities of the poet. When he meets these obligations he proves his poetic integrity:

The poet isn't keeping his word
If he doesn't change the names of things.
. . . .
Every poet with any self respect
Should have his own dictionary

Radical measures like these are unavoidable because

in Parra's presentation of his poetic theory the antipoet is the sole explorer of new literary territory, and the exploration is necessary for the health and survival of the art. He must catalogue the reality that surrounds him and change the old names of things if they are no longer suitable. His duty is to perceive and analyze the real world and to communicate his insights to the reader in the most direct manner possible. If the medium of communication needs to be expanded, altered and revised in order to complete the task, then that is what the antipoet will do even if he must act alone.

Because Parra is the originator of modern antipoetry and a serious humorist, he cannot affect this boastful self-importance for long.[7] He makes himself the target of his own derision, he mocks his own arrogance by studding the grandiose poetic manifesto with prosaic, cliché-ridden expressions, and he offers peculiarly ambiguous examples of the linguistic change he advocates. This deflationary technique, used so effectively and for the same purpose in "Advertencia al lector," accounts for the varieties of language employed in "Cambios de nombre." Colloquial

7. Parra frequently refers to an antipoetic substratum in the history of western culture and generally defines it as a spirt of anticlassicism or antilyricism. In Lerzundi, p. 67, for example, Parra traces antipoetry back to Archilochos, the seventh century Greek poet whom he mistakenly places in the eighth century *B.C.*: "Archilochos . . . had already said the things I have, with a lot of trouble, dared to say now. He totally violated what we would call the lyrical norms of the time; he is an antipoet by way of antonomasia."

words, slang in unexpected places, the solemn cant of the speech writer—the effect of their combination is to undermine the hyperbolic self-importance that the antipoet assigns to himself in the poem. The colloquial expressions are consistent with the generally flat tones of the language used throughout the work, but the obtrusively prosaic phrases like "from now on," "All right, it's been a long night," and "before I forget" heighten the spontaneous effect of Parra's language as well as undercut his pomposity. These phrases are not necessarily comic. Their ironic impact stems from Parra's consistent disregard for belletristic decorum as well as from the incongruity of their presence in a statement of poetic theory. The jargon of "To the lovers of belles-lettres/I send my very best wishes" is more directly humorous. It reverberates with hackneyed, overblown oratory.

Parra's strategy, as an ironic writer, is to force his unwilling hypothetical readers (the despised "lovers of belles-lettres") to accept the abrasive juxtapositions of different levels of language, varieties of tone and bizarre examples of linguistic innovation as the unavoidable facts of the poem. When the belletrists begin to suspect that linguistic experimentation, or rather, hyperbolic pronouncements of intended innovation, may well be the only subject of the work, they are confronted by the unexpected speculation that ends "Cambios de nombre." The final lines, with their parodic theological implications, actually challenge the readers to join the antipoet in the name-changing process and to reconsider the relationship of language to the objects it purportedly describes.

Parra whimsically proposes three incongruous name changes. At first glance they appear to have been selected at random from a multitude of possibilities simply because they seem so irrelevant. They guarantee a comic effect through contrast with the serious purposes of the poem. The first proposal is blatantly absurd: the sun will be called "Pussycat" (the equivalent of Puss-in-Boots). The second combines the names of common objects which have no logical relationship with one another, although "coffins" is certainly a potentially charged allusion. The final, inconclusive conjecture actually requires the reader to reconsider the connection between experiential reality and language. As if he were a medieval theologian, Parra affirms that the varieties of human names that we have devised for God have no necessary relationship to His existence or attributes.

Despite the context of banal language and the mocking tone, Parra clearly intends the examples to be taken as significant statements about antipoetry. Since the first terms of each proposed change ("sun," "shoes," "God") have referents which are tacitly accepted as real within the context of both the poem and of ordinary experience, and since the existence of these referents is independent of any nomenclature devised for them, Parra's role as the antipoet is not only to write of reality (the referents) as any poet would and convey his impressions and interpretations to the reader, but to revise and alter the vocabulary if that is necessary for the sake of improved communication. To Parra's mind belletristic readers can only gain in perception and understanding by allowing their linguistic presuppostions to be shaken, for in all three examples Parra is suggesting that language has no fixed relationship with the referents it describes. In other words, language is a convention so ingrained that it almost seems part of the natural world, but if the reader is willing, the convention—and the tradition behind it—can be broken. The revision of this conventional connection between language and its referents is one of Parra's self-assigned duties as the antipoet. Consequently, "Cambios de nombre" proposes the possibility of changes in the language which are far more radical in their implications than the purely literary ones of "Advertencia al lector" ("rainbow," "sorrow," "torquate" replaced by "chairs and tables," "coffins," "desk accessories"). In this poem Parra is broadening the renovatory impulse to include the language used for ordinary communication. Rather than an altered dictionary he is really advocating a deeper sense of the relationship between speech and experience. Poetry is only one aspect of that relationship and, if he must, the antipoet will leave the necessary name changes up to the reader himself. Obviously, he does not really expect the reader to make any changes at all, but his apparent readiness to let his audience take the lead is a repetition of the challenge to participate in the antipoetic adventure which he issued in "Advertencia al lector." Parra laughs mockingly at his audience by refusing to take a firm position regarding the one

name change that is probably of greatest importance
and interest to most readers. Regardless of who is
finally responsible for the renovation, however, the
matter of primary importance in "Cambios de
nombre" is for both the antipoet and the reader to
realize the potential flexibility of language. It is an
expressive artifact that can describe and give
meaning to other artifacts in the human environment, whether they are ordinary and trivial ("shoes"),
natural and necessary ("sun") or indefinable and ultimately unnameable ("God").

Parra's effort to involve the reader in the exploration of poetic language seems out of phase with other
theories that he develops in his poems on poetry.
First, there is his insistence on the poet's originality
and absolute independence, and his concomitant
refusal to accept responsibility for the uncomfortable
effects his linguistic experimentation may have on
the reader ("Advertencia al lector"). Second, there is
his statement that the duty of the antipoet is to
record and document ordinary, familiar speech in
order to make antipoetry accessible to the very people
whose speech patterns are its raw material ("Manifiesto"). The confusion of the theoretical cul-de-sac
into which Parra joyfully leads us is precisely what
can be expected of the antipoet, who is under no obligation to establish a consistent theoretical system
because his critics, commentators or readers might
require one. Yet no matter what other variations or
permutations of principle occur in these poems, Parra's commitment to familiar, ordinary language is a

constant. This is what accounts for the comfortably colloquial language and the apparent simplicity of the name changes that Parra proposes in "Cambios de nombre." The references are perfectly familiar, and his suggested alterations contain no neologistic or structural surprises. They are composed of, and surrounded by, common words and phrases. Parra is toying with the substitution process and extending it to its ultimate absurdity so that the inane reference to "Pussycat," for example, contrasts vividly with the gravity of the linguistic problems he is dealing with. The statement he makes in "Cambios de nombre," and the means he uses to make it, are incongruous, and the disparity generates a tension that is ironic. That tension is comparable, in the manner in which it is created and in its purpose, to Parra's derisive, deflating treatment of his own exaggerations concerning the weighty significance of his artistic obligations. Parra's ironically ambivalent presentation of serious matters in terms that are essentially comic, and the constant undercutting of his own pomposity in the theoretical poems are examples of what the reader can expect from the antipoet. "Real seriousness is comic," and Parra puts his principle into practice by using humor as the medium for stating his theoretical concerns.

"Manifiesto," as its title indicates, takes the form of a militant statement on the literary and political values of antipoetry. It denounces all that poetry has been but should not be, and proclaims the program of poetic renovation which Parra intends to effect. These ideas are summarized in the twice repeated theme of the poem, which Parra sarcastically designates as his first and final words on the subject: "The poets have come down from Olympus." The abandoned Olympus has twin peaks, one literary and the other political. The rest of the poem explores both areas, condemning the past failures of poetry and exalting its future possibilities.

> Ladies and gentlemen
> This is our final word.
> —Our first and final word—
> The poets have come down from Olympus.
>
> For our elders
> Poetry was a luxury
> But for us
> It is an absolute necessity:
> We cannot live without poetry.
>
> Unlike our elders
> —And I say this with all due respect—
> We maintain
> That the poet is not an alchemist
> The poet is a man like everyone else
> A bricklayer who builds his wall:
> A builder of doors and windows.

We speak
In everyday language
We don't believe in cabalistic signs.

And one other thing:

The poet is there
So that the tree does not grow crooked.

This is our message.
We denounce the demiurge poet
The cheap Bargain Poet
The Bookworm Poet.
All these gentlemen
—And I say this with a lot of respect—
Should be tried and convicted
For having built castles in the air
For having wasted space and time
Writing out their sonnets to the moon
For having grouped words together
    haphazardly
In the latest Parisian style.
Not for us:
Thought is not born in the mouth
It is born in one's heart of hearts.

We repudiate
Dark glasses poetry
Cloak and dagger poetry
Broad-brimmed hat poetry.

We propose instead
Naked eye poetry
Bared bosom poetry
Uncovered head poetry.

We don't believe in nymphs or tritons.
Poetry must be this:
A girl surrounded by wheat
Or it is absolutely nothing.

Well now, in the matter of politics
They, our immediate forebears
Our good, immediate forebears!
Refracted and dispersed themselves
As they passed through the crystal prism.
A few of them became Communists.
I don't know if they were, really.
Let's suppose that they were Communists,
They were not poets of the people
They were respectable bourgeois poets.
We have to tell the truth about things:
Only one or two of them
Knew how to reach the hearts of the people.
Whenever they could
They declared themselves in word and deed
Against committed poetry
Against poetry of the present
Against proletarian poetry.

Let's accept that they were Communists
But their poetry was a disaster

Second hand surrealism
Third hand decadentism
Old wood washed up by the sea.
Adjective poetry
Nasal and guttural poetry
Arbitrary poetry
Poetry copied out of books
Poetry based
On the revolution of the word

"Absolute liberty of expression"

When in fact it should spring
From a revolution of ideas.
Vicious circle poetry
For a half dozen of the elite.

Today we cross ourselves asking
What they wrote those things for
To frighten the petty bourgeois?
Miserable waste of time!
The petty bourgeois only reacts
When it's a question of his stomach.

Imagine frightening him with poems!

The situation is this:
While they were
For a twilight poetry
For a night poetry
We propose

A dawn poetry.
This is our message,
The light of poetry
Must reach everyone equally
Poetry within everyone's grasp.

That's all, comrades
We condemn
—And I really do say this with respect—
The poetry of the little god
The poetry of the sacred cow
The poetry of the furious bull.

Instead of poetry in the clouds
We offer
Poetry on solid ground
—Cold head, warm heart
We are committed to the solid ground—
Instead of cafe poetry
The poetry of nature
Instead of salon poetry
The poetry of the public square
The poetry of social protest.

The poets have come down from Olympus.

Parra's manifesto denounces the poetic tradition by
exaggerating its faults from both a literary and a
political point of view. The disavowal of that tradition
and of the social milieu in which it flourished is of such
a disputatious tone and intention that Parra leaves no

doubt as to why there is an "anti" in antipoetry. The poem, like all manifestoes, is emphatically propagandist. For every poetic vice there is a complementary antipoetic virtue. In "Manifiesto" the affirmations of value are the mirror opposites of the denunciations; together they comprise a determined proclamation of the social and literary merits of the new poetry in direct contrast to wornout custom and usage. Within this context Parra triumphantly defends his own work and celebrates the poets' long-awaited descent from the Olympus of bogus estheticism and bourgeois politics into the world of material and natural necessity. He uses this technique of alternating offensive and defensive tactics (the intentionally warlike terminology is appropriate to a manifesto) to create a militant *apologia pro opera sua*.

Parra describes his writing as the overdue cleaning of poetry's house, as a force which has transformed the poetic art from an anachronistic luxury into an expressive rendering of the daily life and language of common men:

We don't believe in nymphs and tritons.
Poetry must be this:
A girl surrounded by wheat
Or it is absolutely nothing.

This concept of poetry has been one of Parra's constant considerations throughout his literary career, one that he has written about repeatedly. In "Los vicios del mundo moderno" (The Vices of the Modern

World) for example, he states the same idea in very similar terms: "And poetry either resides inside of things or it is no more than a mirage of the spirit." In "Manifiesto," however, he propagandistically over-states his case. Parra exaggerates the defects of the opposition in order to justify his own program of reform. He establishes a causal relationship between the literary and political failings of the past in order to support the claim that his writing can make poetry necessary and significant to ordinary people. The an-tipoet counts himself a member of the proletariat, a creative worker whose labor is poetry but whose needs, aspirations and achievements are no different from those of other workers. His commitment to full poetic solidarity with the other members of the work-ing classes seems eminently Brechtian, but Parra knew none of Brecht's writings early in his career when he was formulating his antipoetic position, and by his own admission has subsequently read little of the German's work. However, like Brecht, Parra is steadfast in his vigorous repudiation of indi-vidualism. Both authors think of what they call in-dividualism in art as a synonym for élitism, and both consider the coterie hateful. Parra has even defined antipoetry as a "collection of masks in which 'I' does not exist," and is enthusiastic about the Dadaist abrogation of the individualized ego in poetry. And, like Brecht, Parra is a stalwart antiromantic who has used his writing to explore and explain human exis-tence. He longs for a poetry that is inseparable from life itself and disclaims interest in any significance or interpretation other than the literal one. He rejects out of hand the "cavalieri della luna" (they are present in "Manifiesto" as the poets who compose "sonnets to the moon") when he states that "the literal meaning is enough for me." He describes his work as a necessary adjunct of ordinary experience: "Poetry can't be anything but life in words. Anything that gives the feel of life to a line is poetry. Antipoetry is an expressive necessity—a necessity of life." Finally, like Brecht, Parra advocates militant communion with the working class through poetry.

In "Manifiesto" the politicization of poetry is evident in the title as well as in the resounding hyperboles of Parra's antibourgeois diatribe against earlier poets. The title of the poem has a double historical connotation that reflects Parra's attack on political and literary irrelevance in the poetic tradition. In literature, it recalls other avant-garde pronouncements, from André Breton's proclamation of a new "anti-rhetoric" to Vicente Huidobro's famous description of himself as the "antipoet." In politics the title suggests the *Communist Manifesto*, especially in light of Parra's criticism of "bourgeois" poetry. The poetic and political militancy suggested by the title is trenchantly emphasized throughout all of "Manifiesto" as the antipoet indicts those poets who live and write as if the practice of their art were the aberrant affliction of an exotic and superior race. His denunciations are a sweeping negation of recent

poetic history. Parra's targets range from the es-
thetes of the coterie to the practitioners of romantic,
post-modernistic and academic verse:

We denounce the demiurge poet
The cheap Bargain Poet
The Bookworm poet
. . . .
We repudiate
Dark glasses poetry
Cloak and dagger poetry
Broad-brimmed hat poetry.
. . . .
We condemn
. . . .
The poetry of the little god
The poetry of the sacred cow
The poetry of the furious bull.

What Parra does advocate in "Manifiesto" is "the
poetry of social protest." The connection between this
idea of poetry and Pablo Neruda's "impure poetry" is
a problematical question. Neruda first used the term
in 1935 and expanded the concept in his purposefully
simplified verse of the early 1950s. Parra has insisted,
repeatedly and vehemently, that the basic elements
of antipoetry—his use of clear, accessible, unmeta-
phorical language to describe ordinary people, objects
and experiences—antedate Neruda's similar concerns
by many years. In 1953, for example, Neruda stated
that his poetry was for "ordinary people, people so

modest that very often they have not learnt to read,"
and he called for a poetry "like bread that can be
shared by all, learned men and peasants alike." [8] But
Parra, in defense of the independent genesis and
development of antipoetry, points to his youthful
rejection of avant-gardism in the late 1930s, to the
importance of Tomás Lago's 1942 prologue "La Luz en
la poesía" (Light in Poetry) as a definition of the
poems that Parra was composing at that time, as well
as to significant antipoems like "La víbora" and "Los
vicios del mundo moderno," which had already been
published in 1948. Still, there is an obvious relationship between the partisan literature which Parra
defends in "Manifiesto" and Neruda's own politicizing poetry. "Manifiesto" was first published in 1963,
not long after Parra's speech in honor of Neruda,
which was published in *Discursos* in 1962. The
similarities between the speech and the poem are
extensive, and even include "El hombre invisible"
(The Invisible Man), the poem by Neruda which Parra
incorporates into his remarks. Both "El hombre invisible" and "Manifiesto" express similar attitudes
toward the social function of the poetic art, attitudes
which are, in turn, practically identical to the position
which Parra takes in *Discursos*. For instance, in his
speech, Parra states that "the essence of Neruda's

8. These remarks are from Neruda's lecture "Obscurity and
Clarity in Poetry" (note the similarity in title to Lago's
prologue) and are cited in English by Michael Hamburger in his
excellent book *The Truth of Poetry* (New York: Harcourt Brace
Jovanovich, 1969) p. 223.

struggle is identical to the struggle of modern man—the move from I to we" (p. 31) and "the *plenitude* of the individual is the natural result of his proper integration into the *social struggle*" (p. 44). And in "Manifiesto" he says:

> The poet is a man like everyone else
> A bricklayer who builds his wall:
> A builder of doors and windows."

In "El hombre invisible" Neruda writes:

> I laugh
> I smile
> at the old poets
> ....
> they always say 'I'
> something happens to them
> every minute
> it's always 'I'
> only they
> or the sweet thing they love
> walk down the streets
> no one else
> ....
> things only happen
> to him
> the poet
> my poor brother
> or to his sweet beloved
> nobody lives

except him alone
nobody cries with hunger
or anger
nobody suffers in his verses
because he can't pay the rent,
in poetry nobody
is thrown out on the street
with his beds and chairs
. . . .
he thinks he is different
from everybody else
. . . .
and so my poor brother
becomes obscure,
he twists and turns
and he is interesting
interesting,
that's the word,
I am not better
than my brother,
but I smile
. . . .
give me
all your joys.
even the most secret ones
. . . .
I must sing them,
give me the everyday
struggle
because that is my song,
and so we will walk together,

shoulder to shoulder,
all men
my song unites them:
the song of the invisible man
who sings with all men.

The two poems present a doctrinaire, left-wing exposition of an ideal poet whose political solidarity
with the masses is directly expressed in his engaged,
socially committed writing. Parra's concise language
contrasts sharply with Neruda's extended discourse,
however, even though "Manifiesto" is one of the
wordiest of the antipoems and Neruda rather arbitrarily breaks his lengthy locutions into the short lines
typical of his *Odas elementales* (Elemental Odes).
Parra clearly follows Neruda's lead in exalting the
political unity that should exist between the poet and
the working classes, but the style and technique of
antipoetry are a different matter. Antipoetry is not
necessarily related to radicalism or a particular political commitment. In fact, the evidence of most of his
other works, and the intrinsic structure of "Manifiesto" itself, do not support Parra's proclamation that
the proletarian cause is the proper standard for
judging poetry.[9]

"Manifiesto" is a dramatic monologue: the manifesto-maker addresses his audience in a very public
voice. The feeling of submerged dialogue in the poem,

9. See Chapter 1, pp. 35-42, for Parra's statements concerning
politics and antipoetry, and for additional discussion of
"Manifiesto."

in which the statements of only one of the interlocu-
tors is recorded, is important for the relationship
which Parra characteristically wishes to establish
between himself and the reader. The reader is included in "Manifiesto" by means of the sardonically
formal "Ladies and gentlemen." The irony implicit in
the creation of this distance between the poet and the
reader in such inappropriate circumstances is tempered toward the end of "Manifiesto" when Parra
refers to his audience as "comrades." The change in
the manner of addressing the reader signifies a
modified attitude toward the reader and the reader's
participation in the aims of the manifesto. In other
words, when Parra uses the term "comrades" he is
allowing his audience to enter the companionable
circle of antipoetic initiates, he is acknowledging the
reader's understanding of the political and literary
matters expounded in the poem, and he is confirming
the sympathy that finally exists between the manifesto-maker and his audience. And yet the relationship between poet and reader is less active in
"Manifiesto" than in either "Cambios de nombre"
or "Advertencia al lector." In these poems Parra delights in enticing the reader into the action of the
poem so that he will share in the consequences of the
antipoetic venture. In "Manifiesto," on the other
hand, Parra's expression of comradeship with the
reader only appears after the militantly political
portions of the poem with their pointed denunciations of the older poets and their bourgeois loyalties
and esthetics.

The grammar of "Manifiesto" also belies Parra's declared position as an activist poet. The modulation of dry, ironic formality into comradely intimacy— when the "ladies and gentlemen" turn into "comrades" —is reflected in an analogous range of verb forms used in the denunciations and pronouncements of the manifesto. Most of the verbs, with their corollary pronouns and possessives, are first-person plurals. They can be classified as "exclusive" or "inclusive" on the basis of their relationship to the reader: do they exclude him from or include him in the action expressed by the verb. Phrases like "our final word," "we maintain," and "we repudiate" are examples of the exclusive verb forms that characterize the poem. The "we" is editorial, and "I" could easily be substituted for it. All but two of the first person plural verbs appear to indicate communal action, but in fact express individual action. Conversely, the inclusive verb forms draw the reader into the action and oblige him to participate in the assumptions and speculations of the antipoet. The two inclusive instances concern the alleged political loyalties of the poets: "Let's suppose that they were Communists" and "Let's accept that they were Communists." The joint activity of the manifesto-maker and his silent audience is restricted to the overtly political and strongly propagandist middle section of the poem. The placement of these verbs could be thought of as preparation for the significant change of address that follows, but "comrades" echoes hollowly in the context of exclusive, editorial verbs with their implications of self-assertiveness. Parra's occasional and limited comradeship with his readers cannot withstand the overwhelming individualism of his grammar. The public is included directly in the action of the poem only twice, and only twice do the verbal structures conform to the community of interest and radically political view of poetry heralded in "Manifiesto." Parra even uses a first-person singular verb form for his most acerbic and ironic remarks about the politics and literary achievements of his predecessors: "I say this with all due respect," for example. The tension between the purely individualized first-person verbs on the one hand, and the exclusive and inclusive first-person plural verbs on the other, reiterates the ambiguity of Parra's attitudes toward his social role as a creative writer. The gamut of verb forms, in other words, is comparable to the range of theoretical notions that Parra presents in his poems about poetry. He defends poetry as a communal art in which the poet records the social artifact of language, and he defends with equal vigor the concept of the artist as the originator and adventurous creator of a new poetic language. There is probably no way out of Parra's theoretical labyrinth except to recall his own statement that the antipoet reserves the right to make contradictory formulations whenever he pleases.

The puzzling disparities of Parra's position concerning the political duties of the poet are compounded by the evidence of the antipoems themselves. Despite the proclamations of "Manifiesto" few of his works are straightforward political statements.

Many antipoems comment on the absurdities and tragedies that the individual encounters in society, but these sad, ironic, comic, essentially moralizing observations of human frailty are satiric rather than political. Parra defines political poetry in "Manifiesto" as the "poetry of social protest," and only six of his poems, all from *Emergency Poems*, conform to his rather doctrinaire and restrictive definition. "Inflación" (Inflation) is an overt exposition of the economic contradictions of capitalism. "Sigmund Freud" is in many respects a companion poem to "Manifiesto" in which Parra contrasts the virtues of the People's Republic of China with an absurd and decadent West. "Señora" (Madam) is a satire that attacks the middle class' limited comprehension of the pathetic restrictions of poverty. "Viva Stalin" (Long Live Stalin) describes political murder, although the character of the narrator in the poem is delineated in a somewhat ambivalent fashion. Similarly, "Como dice Marcuse" (As Marcuse Says) comments, although ambiguously, on the current political situation. Finally there is "Pasatiempos" (Pastimes), a poem which seems extremely subjective, but whose anarchic references ultimately resolve into an attack on political violence, both of the left and of the right. Other antipoems have political overtones, but they express no firm political commitment or position, and cannot be considered literature of "social protest." Even when Parra portrays Che Guevara sympathetically in "Como les iba diciendo" (As I Was Saying), or attacks an anti-Communist

ex-president of Chile, González Videla, in "Los
límites de Chile" (The Borders of Chile), or alludes to
the Pentagon, Cuba and the problem of pollution in
"Tiempos modernos" (Modern Times), his politics are
invariably tempered by an overwhelmingly personal
and subjective sense of humor, satire, despair or fu-
tility that removes works like these from the arena of
militant social action described in "Manifiesto." Parra
is indeed engaged, but not in the direct social protest
he advocates in this poem.

"Manifiesto" does not deal exclusively with a theory
of social relevance in literature, however. Parra also
includes the apolitical criteria of normalcy and
necessity. In many respects Parra's theory of poetry
as a form of social protest is a circumstantial outgrowth of these two standards of judgment. Antipoetry, as it is described in "Manifiesto," is ordinary
and found everywhere—like the people whose experience it attempts to express.

Antipoetry documents the familiar language
known to everyone in their daily conversation.
Because it is commonplace and easily recognizable, it
is actually a written manifestation of normal speech.
This concept is diametrically opposed to the élitist
notion that poetry is really a closed or obscure form of
discourse different from ordinary speech. Parra reiterates the point throughout the poem:

> ... the poet is not an alchemist,
> The poet is a man like everyone else
>
> . . . .

We speak
In everyday language
We don't believe in cabalistic signs.

Although Parra frequently uses traditional meters in his compositions, his ideal is to reproduce the vocabulary, feeling and cadences of spoken language in his writing. Parra believes that the poet must "capture the rhythm of speech" and use the unadorned idiom without regard to sonorities: "Music keeps the poet from realizing his fundamental purpose, which has to do with being, not with sounds." Parra thinks of antipoetry as an effort to establish direct communication with the reader by using the reader's own spoken language as its medium, and he calls his writing the force that can liberate verse from "the tyranny of metaphorical expression." Directly related to these ideas is Parra's disavowal of poetry as a lyrical showcase for the poet's ego and his rejection of a poetic language that differs syntactically, figuratively or imagistically from normal conversational speech. Whether the creative artist can consistently remove himself from his individual perception and interpretation of experiential data and achieve total objectivity as well as a complete merging of himself with the mass is too problematical and extensive a question, and one too metaphysical in its implications, to be resolved here. But depersonalized poetry is clearly one of Parra's artistic goals. Although depersonalization often appears to be synonymous with the deromanticization of literature, it is a natural concomitant to his ideas concerning ordinary language in poetry.

Another related concept is the necessity of poetry. This is repeated throughout "Manifiesto," and is an extension of Parra's commitment to the use of normal language in his writing. Specifically, he rejects all notions of poetry which make it a luxury of the privileged or a salon entertainment removed from the natural and social necessities of the real world:

> For our elders
> Poetry was a luxury
> But for us
> It is an absolute necessity:
> We cannot live without poetry.
> . . . .
> The poet is there
> So that the tree does not grow crooked.

Parra speaks of antipoetry as enormously significant in the struggle for human survival in a hostile, chaotic world, but only if the poet makes a direct confrontation with what he has seen and felt. He must avoid the barriers of obscure "poetic" considerations that can stand between himself and his perception, between himself and the public he writes for, between himself and the intrinsic value of his art and the universal need for it. This, more than the limitations of "social protest," is the real meaning of the motif phrase "The poets have come down from Olympus."

In "Advertencia al lector," "Cambios de nombre" and "Manifiesto," Parra forges his literary theories into the materials and themes of his poetry. He reaches specific conclusions concerning the nature and purpose of antipoetry and his own function as its creator. "Manifiesto" stands out from Parra's general treatment of poetic principles because it insists upon political considerations not contained in the other two poems, but in many respects the ideal of social relevance and protest which it expresses is an extension of or a variation on the antipoet's continuing disavowal of élitism in literature. The difference between antipoetry and the tradition of modern poetry—what amounts essentially to romanticism, symbolism, modernism and avant-gardism and their special forms of obscurity—is treated as a linguistic problem in "Cambios de nombre" and "Advertencia al lector." In "Manifiesto" the question of differences is imbued with political overtones, but the matter of primary and fundamental importance is still the contrast between "poetic" and "antipoetic" forms of expression. In all three poems Parra differentiates between the two dictions, comparing them and suggesting that every poetic thesis (defect) has its antipoetic antithesis (virtue).

The aim of antipoetry is to cut away the poetic accretions—specially charged words, obscure vocabulary, imagery and metaphors—and to free and simplify literary language by returning it to the popular roots of the spoken idiom. Parra takes varying and sometimes contradictory positions on how this is to be accomplished. He presents antipoetry as the result of mutual cooperation between the poet and the reader, or as the construct of an autonomous creator, or as a documentary record of commonplace street language. Despite the contradictions, however, he consistently advocates the renovation and renewal of poetic process and materials. He proposes simplifying and clarifying poetic language by ignoring all considerations of beauty, sonority or belletristic decorum. He is committed without exception to this vision of the poetic function: the poet must perceive reality, rationally apprehend it and communicate his perception to the reader by galvanizing him into sharing both the understanding and the perception. In order to achieve this shock of recognition in comtemporary society the poet must employ the real language of real people. Any other discourse defeats the purpose of poetry because any other discourse is alien to the reader. Others before him have recognized that literature becomes rarified and exotic as it moves away from ordinary speech, but Parra has carried these ideas further than any other poet writing in Spanish. His program for linguistic renovation may well embrace political factors, but the call for active political solidarity with the masses in "Manifiesto" is essentially another version of his repeated challenge to the reader to participate in the linguistic explorations of antipoetry. Political militancy is subordinate to the linguistic militancy which is the pervading concern of the poems on poetry.

Parra's theoretical speculations are tempered by a

characteristic irony which is evident even in his most serious statements of the value of antipoetry and the importance of his experiments with language. For example, he establishes sardonically formalized relations with the reader although he simultaneously invites his audience to participate in the antipoetic adventure. He not only condemns older poetry for its failure to communicate, its élitism and its irrelevance, but he delights in sarcastically exaggerating all its defects. Except in "Manifiesto," one of the few antipoems where he evidently forgets that "real seriousness is comic," Parra even directs his ironic barbs against his own inflated self-importance and undercuts his rather pompous proclamations of poetic theory with incongruous language and references. Yet his detractors are satirized so skillfully that apparent censure is transformed into a praise and defense of antipoetry.

What emerges, then, from these theoretical poems, is Parra's determination to goad the reader until he shares the poet's responses to human existence. He views that goal as the most important function of poetry, and believes that only the ordinary spoken language, bare of "poetic" overtones and anachronisms, can communicate clearly and deeply enough to achieve that end.

CHAPTER III

The Technique
of Antipoetry

The fundamental question that needs to be resolved in any approach to Parra's technique is why he invariably uses the glaringly prosaic discourse that characterizes antipoetry. There are two primary reasons for the consistent presence of colloquialisms and clichés in his writing. One grows directly out of Parra's continuing commitment to familiar, popular speech as his expressive and descriptive medium; this consideration has been discussed in Chapter 2, "The Theory of Antipoetry." The other is intimately related to Parra's ironic and comic purposes. When Parra uses banal language and humorous turns of phrase in compositions that are essentially tragic or pathetic, he creates an irony so pervasive that it determines important elements of structure in many of the antipoems.

Language that is not emotively congruous with the subject matter is a basic component of the structure of antipoetry. The ironic effect of prosaic language in this context underscores the differing points of view of the poem's protagonist and the reader who observes him, emphasizes the disparities between the tone of the work and its intention and highlights the tensions between connative and denotative statements which result from those disparities. Parra wants the reader to sense the incongruity and respond to the disparate emotional tones in antipoetry. He calls his writing a poetry of "affective tones that contrast with one another" [1] and he aphoristically describes the technique of antipoetry as one compounded of simultaneous "laughter and tears." The theoretical poems—"Advertencia al lector," for example—are documents of the delight he takes in discordant juxtapositions of serious, weighty matter and slang-ridden, banal language. The affective tones of antipoetry are the product of the intentionally inconsistent system of signs which Parra creates within each poem.

The imagery, the figures, the serious, comic, ordinary or exalted feeling of the language in a poem, the statement or perception which the poet communicates to the reader and the uniform or disparate manner in which all of these elements work together constitute a system of signs and emotive signals to

1. Julio Ortega, "Nicanor Parra y las paradojas," *MNuP.* no. 11 (1967), p. 90.

the reader. The signals stimulate a visceral response that depends upon both the nature of each element in the sign system and whether each element is congruous or incongruous with all the others. If the response which a poet desires to stimulate and his poetic statement have an emotive tone and effect that is comparable to the various elements which produce that statement, then the sign system is straightforward and direct and the affective texture of a poem is harmonious and classically decorous.[2] In compositions with a uniform sign system there is a relatively smooth and continuous development of the theme and a steady, almost predictable movement toward its conclusion. Parra, however, creates an inconsistent sign system in the antipoems. He uses comic clichés and banalities when he writes of despair and exploits the burlesque and parodic possibilities inherent in prosaic language, but behind the comically ironic mask he is in dead earnest. He intends to join the disparities, to treat pathetic themes as if they were humorous, forging a link between inconsistent signs by equating their affective impact and making a new antipoetic synthesis out of the incongruities. Parra has summarized the motivating force behind this synthesizing process with a typically sardonic and epigrammatic statement: "I think that the poet should be a specialist in communication. Humor makes contact [with the reader] easier. Remember

2. See Rosemond Tuve, *Elizabethan and Metaphysical Imagery*, Phoenix Books (Chicago: University of Chicago Press, 1961), esp. chap. IX, "The Criterion of Decorum."

that it's when you lose your sense of humor that you begin to reach for your pistol" (Skarmeta, p. 38).

In antipoetry the most common objects—telephones, soda fountains, park benches, even the colloquial language in which the poems are written —although they are the ordinary artifacts of modern urban life, are charged with desperate significance. They become the hostile furniture of quotidian existence that stands in the way of the protagonists and prevents them from making any heroic gestures because their environment, habits and background render such gestures ludicrous:

> I give no one the right.
> I worship a piece of rag.
> I transport coffins.
>
> I transport coffins.
> I give no one the right.
> I look ridiculous
> In the sunlight,
> Scourge of the soda fountains
> I am dying of fury.

> ("Rompecabezas" [Puzzle])

Yet the inhabitants of the antipoetic world—the personae of the poems—suffer, on the deepest level, the agonizing puzzles of aging, the passage of time and love, the inevitable confrontation with death and the bewildering realization that one becomes conscious of beauty and youth and potentiality only when one is losing them. Their feelings are universal, and profound, and familiar, but the expressive possibilities of the antipoetic protagonists strain against the verbal limitations of an experience that furnishes their world with taxis and boarding houses. It humiliates them with bleeding noses:

> I don't know how I wound up here
> I was running happy and content
> With my hat in my right hand
> After a phosphorescent butterfly
> Who drove me wild with joy
>
> When suddenly pow! I tripped
> And I don't know what happened to the
>   garden
> The landscape changed completely!
>
> My mouth and nose are bleeding.
>
> Really I don't know what happened
> Save me once and for all
> Or shoot me in the back of the neck.
>
> ("Socorro!" [Help!])

It torments them with unheroic ailments:

. . . .

> The fact is that I feel bad
> That same pain in my stomach
> And the constant dizzy feeling.

What do you mean bad: I feel great!
I've never felt better in my life!
I only wish I could feel terrible!

Look carefully and you will see
That I can't stop laughing.

("Saranguaco" [Hodgepodge])

They live anguished lives which seem pathetic because their bellyaches and bloody noses are, from a "poetic" point of view, inappropriate to a tragic figure. Then too, the banal vocabulary of popular song lyrics, the glaring shorthand of journalistc sentimentality, overripe clichés and jargon are the blunted means of communication that the protagonists use in their invariably deficient effort to verbalize their suffering and despair. Even the antipoetic characters' self-defining concepts of themselves and their experiences are limited by the sentimental vocabulary and banal language of the mass culture. The irony of antipoetry is born of the union of an individualized, suffering consciousness with a remarkably prosaic language and gesture. Rodríguez Monegal (in Aguirre and Palazuelos, p. 12), calls this the "deliberately colloquial . . . bureaucratic information" that is typical of the antipoetic style. Parra uses it to affect the reader by reexposing him, in an unexpected context, to the language he hears and may well use every day:

It is with great satisfaction
That I take advantage of this marvelous
    opportunity
Made available to me by the science of death
To clarify a few issues. . . .

("Lo que el difunto dijo de sí mismo"
["What the Dead Man Said about Himself"])

The challenge for the antipoet is to achieve two different artistic effects simultaneously, and to make these opposites complementary. On the one hand, Parra modulates the tensions between the prosaic and tragic elements within the same work and creates the synthesis of comedy and pathos. This is an essential factor in the distinctive affective texture of antipoetry. But he also manipulates and emphasizes the tension between the opposing emotive signals to the reader. In other words, he stresses the differences between the prosaic, comic signs and the tragic, pathetic signs so that the reader is constantly aware of their ironic incompatibility. Parra then incorporates the reader into the ironic structure itself by using our perception of disparity as an intrinsic part of that structure. Parra intends that the reader's sense of the differences between the protagonist's banal language and the emotional misery huddled behind his clichés produce a feeling of ironic distance between himself, the observer of the protagonist and the created persona who lives and speaks each poem. The language in each poem has a comic effect that lies well within our grasp. Because it is easily accessible to the reader it is directly responsible for the psychic separation of the observer from the protagonist, who invariably has a witless, inept response to the poetic situation. The reader is affected by the comic tone of the poem (its denotation) at variance with its presentation of a distraught emotional state (its connotation).

Carlos Bousoño, the Spanish critic, makes no reference to Parra in his book *Teoría de la expresión poética* (A Theory of Poetic Expression), 3a ed. (Madrid: Editorial Gredos, 1962), but in Chapter XII, "La poesía y la comicidad" (Poetry and the Comic), his discussion of the inherent differences between comedy and poetry not only clarifies the antipoetic process, but also seems to give a theoretical and objective justification for Parra's use of the term antipoetry. Bousoño cites Bergson's formula "Laughter arises from the contemplation of something mechanical or rigid injected into what is living" (p. 285), and then he elucidates that basic statement: ". . . every joke makes us perceive a certain awkwardness, a rigidity or mechanization in the spirit or body of another human being. . . ." (pp. 288-289). Bousoño goes on to compare two kinds of figurative language and finds that in general disparity typifies the comic phenomenon, while decorum is characteristic of the poetic. His remarks are an enlightening contribution to the definition of antipoetic irony: ". . . the poet wants the objects united in the image to bear a maximum resemblance to each other (either physically or emotively), to coincide as much as possible in an intrinsic, fundamental way. The comic writer, on the contrary, avoids strong analogy and tries to achieve minimal resemblance: the comic metaphor occurs when two objects which resemble one another very little are presented as equivalent" (pp. 292-293). Finally, Bousoño asserts that the reader's perception of rigid or mechanized responses in the protagonist (in other words, his perception of disparity and inadequacy) is the source of the comic, as opposed to the lyrical or decorous phenomenon (the italics are Bousoño's): "*The reader . . . perceives the spiritual reality of the subject as unsuitable or inappropriate to the circumstances.* It is a reality that would not exist if the subject were in accord with the life around him or with his own life, if the texture of his soul were not overly rigid. . . . We *accept* a poetic content; we do not accept a comic one, but we do *tolerate* it, since the 'error' manifested there is produced by an easily recognizable cause. . . . Poetry and jokes are two sides of the same coin, the two poles of a sphere. The opposite of poetry is not 'prose' in the sense of unpoetic diction. *The opposite of poetry is the joke*" (pp. 296-297).

Bousoño's definition of comedy can be applied to antipoetry in this way: when the reader carries the suggestions, statements and incongruities of the antipoem to their logically emotive conclusion, he can intuit the restrictive, tortuous situation which is at the root of the persona's suffering, and then interpret his predicament differently from the protagonist. The

irony which results is situational: at once burlesque
and pathetic, it is concurrent with the sense of distance between the persona, who describes and reacts
to his circumstance, and the reader who, in his own
eyes, makes a more sensitive and insightful interpretation of the poetic situation. Parra insists on the
distance between them. The irony produced by their
different perceptions of the same situation—that is,
the situational irony—causes the reader to view the
persona's ineffectual and automatic responses with a
mixture of scorn, pity and amusement. The reader's
feelings of inappropriate but irresistible amusement,
even though the protagonist's suffering surely calls
for compassion, is central to the ironic structure of the
antipoems in which the reader seems to have more
insight than the protagonist. As if the antipoem were
an epistolary novel in which we know and perceive
vastly more than at least one of the correspondents,
much of the bitter humor of antipoetry stems from
this basic ironic situation: we are in on the joke while
the victim, the protagonist, is innocent of its implications or helpless to do anything about them:

. . . .
I a born delinquent
Caught infraganti
Stealing flowers by the light of the moon
I beg the whole world's pardon
But I do not admit that I am guilty

("Yo pecador" [I a Sinner]

The tensions which are created by the contrast between the protagonist's partial awareness and our seemingly more complete awareness place the reader in a position of apparent superiority, for he prides himself on his high level of consciousness, his sensitivity to the subtle emotional ramifications of the poetic situation and his intuitive knowledge that lies far beyond the protagonist's capacities. In Baudelaire's words: ". . . there will be found in the mental attitude of the one who laughs, a certain unconscious sense of pride . . . the essence of the comic is . . . the development in the spectator, or in the reader, of a delighted consciousness of his own superiority. . . ." [3] We can respond to the prosaic denotations of the poem with amusement and even apprehend the fitting compassionate response to its moving connotations, but the persona is limited by the restrictions of his linguistic and emotional experience and reacts to his despair with inadequate banalities. The reader's initial response—his belief that this is *comic* poetry—grows out of his perception of an everwidening and comforting distance between himself and the protagonist whose words and gestures are consistently inappropriate to the circumstances that cause his suffering. The pathetic *connotations* of the poem, juxtaposed to the familiar, shallow or absurd language and data of daily life

3. Charles Baudelaire, *The Essence of Laughter and Other Essays, Journals and Letters*, ed. Peter Quennel (New York: Meridian Books, 1956), pp. 116, 130. Subsequent references will be included in the text.

that are the poem's ironic *denotations*, are the components of the antipoetic synthesis which galvanize us into an uncommon response to the common language of the antipoem. In other words, the emotional impact of antipoetry is created in spite of, not because of, the elements that Parra employs to make his statements. The explicit statements of each antipoem are almost never consonant with the implicit meaning of the composition. We perceive the incongruity and are amused.

But the reader experiences a subsequent reaction which intensifies and compounds the ironic structure and is necessary for the fulfillment of the poet's intention. Parra makes certain that the language is ordinary, the circumstances familiar and the backgrounds commonplace. And indeed, they are ordinary, familiar and commonplace because they are the same as the reader's. They are the unavoidable facts of urban living and the component elements of our own quotidian experience. When the reader realizes this—when he hears his own favorite cliché in the mouth of the protagonist, for example—he also realizes that he has been deceived in his feeling of superiority. We shamefacedly have to accept that our responses would probably be the same as the protagonist's if we were in his situation. At this moment the ironic distance begins to close, the reader stops being the removed, superior observer of the protagonist and becomes instead his Baudelairean twin and brother, taking on the shape, form and reponses of the poetic persona. The multiple points of view that contributed to the ironic structure and account for much of the humor in antipoetry become a single point of view as the observer and the protagonist merge into one suffering identity.

The desperate quandary that amuses us because it is not ours, and moves us to a not unpleasurable, somewhat scornful compassion for the pathetic protagonist, lacks the awesome cathartic quality that we might hope for in the medium that has become the poetic expression of our own feelings and situation. The language and gesture that the reader now sees as his own may be ignoble, banal and even comic, yet they indicate a deeply felt struggle against the powerful restrictions of our human condition. Parra forces us, in the embarrassing company of his protagonist, into the unenviable position of Everyman. Parra's purposes approximate the sardonic, all-embracing denunciations of a moralist, for the weaknesses, frustrations and unheroic despair revealed in the clichés and prosaic jargon of the antipoems are the "sins" of the reader as well as of the protagonist. The ineptitudes, failures and foolishness of his antihero are achingly familiar. The banalities of his linguistic, gestural and emotional reponses chagrin us because they are the mirror image of our own ineffectual language and bewildered gesture when we are confronted by the vast mortifications of our condition.

The irony of the initial distance between reader and persona is compounded by their eventual identification. The inferior perceptions and attenuated sensitivity of the protagonist, counted on by the reader as a guarantee of his own self-esteem, is chimerical. Our half-contemptuous laughter at the expense of the protagonist becomes an integral part of the structural irony when we are unwillingly made aware of our pathetic fusion with him: "Laughter, they say, comes of superiority . . . laughter is, to some extent, a symptom of weakness. Indeed, what more obvious sign of debility can there be than the nervous convulsion . . . provoked by somebody else's misfortune. . . . What spectacle can be more deplorable than that of weakness rejoicing at weakness?" (Baudelaire, pp. 115–116).

The complex antipoetic structure is the crucial center of the textual analyses that follow. The works I discuss with this structure in mind are prototypical antipoems and models of the ironic process which, to varying degrees, is present in most of Parra's writing. These paradigmatic examples of antipoetry are from *Poemas y antipoemas* and are thematically and technically interrelated, although the ironic technique that unites them is not confined to that collection or these poems.

"Preguntas a la hora del té" (Questions at Teatime), "Notas de viaje" (Travel Notes), "El peregrino" (The Pilgrim), "Recuerdos de juventud" (Memories of Youth), "El túnel" (The Tunnel), "La víbora" (The Viper) and "La trampa" (The Trap) form a thematic unit. The seven poems make similar poetic statements, and despite obvious variations they are closely related to each other through identical syntax, referents and imagery. Except for the first ("Preguntas a la hora del té"), which is a preface to the thematic unit rather than an intrinsic part of it, the poems constitute the confessions of a poetic persona whom Parra identifies as "I." In my discussion all references are to the persona and not to the man.

The poems recall a period in the past when the protagonist is completely cut off from meaningful emotional and physical contact with the rest of the world. His extreme isolation is manifested as obscurity in his writing:

> I spent the nights at my desk
> Absorbed in the practice of automatic writing
> > ("El túnel")

as metaphysical speculations:

> Is the transparent glass superior
> To the hand of the man who creates it?
> > ("Preguntas a la hora del té")

as barren relations with other people:

> People laughed at my sudden fits
> Individuals shook in their armchairs like algae
> > moved by the waves
> And women gave me hate-filled looks
> > > ("Recuerdos de juventud")

and as symptoms of a total spiritual and bodily malaise:

A soul that has been bottled up for years
In a kind of sexual and intellectual abyss
Barely feeding himself through the nose
Wants you to listen to him
                                        ("El peregrino")

His wasteland has a beginning and an ending, and follows a definite pattern. He is involuntarily seduced into a figurative prison, often by a woman or women. The prison is alternately conceived of, in concrete symbolic terms, as a tunnel, a trap, an abyss, a bottle, a ship's cabin, a round room, a house. Regardless of its form, he is enclosed in the prison and stumbles through it. He simultaneously knocks into the people and objects of the real world, but has no relation to them. He sometimes calls for help, but is not heard or understood, and is shunned for his absurd remarks. Exhausted by the trivial or venal activities he is obliged to engage in, he eventually moves toward an escape, but at great cost to his vital energies. The imprisonment evoked in the poems primarily symbolizes a self-imposed social and literary isolation, and a devastating sexual and emotional crisis. Parra merges the problems of the public and the private selves to render a complete portrait of an alienated, suffering personality, yet despite the profound seriousness of the theme—the self lost and the hope of the self regained—it is presented in the ironic, parodic, ordinary language of antipoetry.

Because it is a concise and direct statement of the basic problems which are the root causes of the protagonist's suffering, "Preguntas a la hora del té" can serve as an introduction to the thematic unit.

This pale gentleman seems like
A figure in the wax museum;
He looks through the torn curtains:
What is worth more, gold or beauty?
Is the moving stream worth more
Or the immobile grass on the bank?
In the distance a bell is heard
That opens one more wound, or closes it:
Is the water in the fountain more real
Or the girl who looks at herself in it?
No one knows, people pass him by
Building castles in the sand.
Is the transparent glass superior
To the hand of the man who creates it?

One breathes a tired air
Of ashes, of smoke, of sadness:
What was once seen is not seen again
The same way, say the dry leaves.
Time for tea, toast, margarine,
Everything enveloped in a kind of fog.

The nostalgic, depressed tone of the poem is consistent with its restrained style. Although the references and vocabulary are banal, the familiar language is free of comically charged clichés, and a trite phrase like "a kind of" has a conversational rather than a humorous effect. The irony in this fairly early work (it is from Section I of *Poemas y antipoemas)* lies not so much in the language used to present the protagonist's metaphysical speculations as in the contrast between the dreary, desolate background and the platonistic "questions" that preoccupy him as he ponders the problems of movement as opposed to permanence, the temporal as opposed to the eternal, art as opposed to the artisan. The problems are old and insoluble, and "enveloped in a kind of fog." The sense of cerebral waste is matched by the dying season ("dry leaves"), the protagonist's unhealthy pallor and his isolation from the outside world which he looks at "through the torn curtains" as "people pass him by."

The problems of solitary withdrawal from the real world into an enclosure and of inadequate response to the world are summarized in "Preguntas a la hora del té," and Parra clearly states their cause. His protagonist perceives reality incompletely because his vision is hampered by a cloudy mysticism which is symbolized by the torn curtain. His philosophical preoccupations seem tired and meaningless because the symbol for them is ludicrously trivial and ordinary when compared to the protagonist's ponderous speculations. The six poems of the thematic unit enlarge upon this theme, dealing with it in varying contexts but with comparable ironic emphasis.

The rhetorical figures of indirect vision and enclosure, which represent the imprisonment of the protagonist, are treated in much greater detail in "El túnel," where Parra provides more specific information about his alienated antihero:

> I spent a period of my youth in the house of
>   some aunts
> Because of the death of a gentleman who had
>   been an intimate friend of theirs
> And whose ghost annoyed them mercilessly
> Making their life impossible.
> At first I was deaf to their telegrams
> To their letters written in the language of
>   another time
> Full of mythological allusions
> And the proper names of people I knew
>   nothing about
> Some of them belonged to ancient wise men
> To second rate medieval philosophers
> Or simply to people in the neighborhood
>   where they lived.
>
> Leaving the university just like that
> Breaking with the charms of the gallant life
> Interrupting everything
> Just to satisfy the whims of three hysterical
>   old women

Full of all kinds of personal problems
Seemed, to a person like me, to be
A not very attractive future
A mad idea.

Nevertheless, I lived in The Tunnel for four
    years,
In close proximity to those fearful ladies
Four years of constant martyrdom
Martyrdom day and night.
The hours of happiness I spent under the
    trees
Soon turned into weeks of boredom
Into months of anguish which I did my best to
    hide
So as not to arouse curiosity about myself.
They turned into years of ruin and misery
Into centuries of imprisonment that my soul
    endured
Inside a bottle on the table!

My spiritualist conception of the world
Put me in a position of absolute inferiority
    when confronted by real facts:
I saw everything through a prism
At the bottom of which the images of my
    aunts wove in and out like living threads
Forming a kind of impenetrable armor
That wounded my vision and made it more and more
    ineffective.

A young man of limited means doesn't know
   about things.
He lives in a bell jar called Art
Called Lust, called Science
Trying to make contact with a world of
   relationships
That only exist for him and a small group of
   friends.

Under the effects of a kind of water vapor
That filtered in through the floor of my room
And filled the air and made everything
   invisible
 I spent my nights at my desk
Absorbed in the practice of automatic writing.

But why go any further into these unpleasant
   matters
Those matrons made a miserable fool of me
With their false promises, their strange
   fantasies
Their skillfully simulated sorrows
They managed to keep me in their nets for
   years
Tacitly obliging me to work for them
Doing agricultural chores
And buying and selling animals
Until one night, looking through the keyhole
I realized that one of them
My paralyzed aunt!

Could walk perfectly well on tiptoe
And I came back to reality with a goddamn
    awful feeling.

Almost without realizing it the protagonist is drawn
into the ambience of his "aunts." During an un-
specified time of his youth he enters their figurative
tunnel where he remains for "four years of constant
martyrdom," and his "hours of happiness" are transformed into "weeks of boredom," "months of anguish," "years of ruin and misery" and "centuries of
imprisonment." This seemingly endless time of misery and alienation is expressed in two basic tropes,
both of which evoke the image of faulty perception
and imprisonment. One refers to glass as the barrier
between the protagonist and the world, the other alludes to a misty vapor that clouds his vision, obscures
his surroundings and is really a second barrier
between himself and reality. Beginning with the title
of the poem, the images of enclosure are "Inside a
bottle on the table," "in a bell jar," and "they managed to keep me in their nets." The images of faulty
perception are closely related to the figure of imprisonment: "I saw everything through a prism," "The
images of my aunts wove in and out like living
threads/Forming a kind of impenetrable armor/That
wounded my vision and made it more and more ineffective." Not all the prisons are of glass: the tunnel
and the net also enclose him. Glass not only imprisons
him, but affects his vision as well: he sees "everything
through a prism."

Parra expresses the isolation of the protagonist in concrete terms and specifies the nature of his imprisonment by clearly identifying its causes. Both the persona and his aunts are to blame for his enclosure, because both the young man and the old women share attitudes that inevitably lead to psychic, social and literary isolation. Every interpretative signal to the reader concerning the characters of the protagonist and his aunts is presented as an image of imprisonment or defective vision. For example, the first indication of his personality is also the first allusion to the imprisonment:

> ... I did my best to hide
> So as not to arouse curiousity about myself

The protagonist consciously presents a false front to the world, but once he is locked into the subterfuge he discovers that the acceptable appearance is transformed into a prison as inevitably as the "months of anguish" turn into "centuries of imprisonment."

The protagonist's "spiritualist conception of the world" is intimately connected to his alienation; this phrase introduces the lines that describe the total distortion of his visual perceptions and which indicate the real causative relationship between his failed ability to perceive, his enclosure and the three old women:

> I saw everything through a prism
> At the bottom of which the images of my

aunts wove in and out like living threads
Forming a kind of impenetrable armor
That wounded my vision and made it more
   and more ineffective.

He becomes more and more involuted as he with-
draws into abstractions, metaphysical speculations
and the obscure literary pleasures of the avant-garde.
The three aunts may well represent the various manifestations of his isolation in the tunnel: the denial of
his true self, the belief in a world of the spirit,
the practice of automatic writing that searches for
meaning in the individual unconscious and not in
social relationships. In any case, they are fraudulent
and deceptive. They are "hysterical" and "fearful"
old women who catch him in their nets, distort his
perceptions and, worst of all, keep him prisoner in
their tunnel under false pretenses. From the very
beginning of the poem they weave the enclosure of
isolation around the protagonist until he becomes an
almost willing prisoner in the tunnel. The feeling of
hysterical, willful guile begins with the first allusion
to a dead past in their initial communications with
him and finally blossoms into his discovery that the
allegedly paralyzed aunt is walking around on tiptoe.
His sudden, brusque contact with reality is depicted
as a clearing of his vision, although it ironically occurs
when he squints his eyes to peep through a keyhole.
The immediate result is that he is freed from the
clutches of the old women and from the tunnel in
which he had been enclosed. But it is not a joyous

escape. Despite the misery and boredom in the tunnel, it gives him a "goddamn awful feeling" to have to confront his freedom again. As Parra says in the poem "Inflación" (Inflation):

Inside the cage there is food.
Not much, but some.
Outside there are only vast stretches of
    liberty.

Parra does not give any information about the world outside the tunnel, but it is reasonable to assume that it contains the opposite of all he found inside the prison—the tedious abstractions, the hidden and obscure relationships among things and ideas, the retreat to the coterie in his writings—in short, all the deformations of reality that can be subsumed under the rubric a "spiritualist conception of the world."

"El peregrino" presents another aspect of the protagonist's isolation. In this poem he wanders aimlessly and makes unsuccessful attempts at reaching out to the rest of the world for physical and spiritual contact. He is, however, still imprisoned and discovers in despair that there is still no link to the world for him, for he is ignored by its inhabitants, and the trap is unchanged. Ironically, the rhetorical figure that expresses his isolation is one of simultaneous pilgrimage and imprisonment. Parra has called the first six lines a burlesque invocation to the muse, after

which "the poet becomes serious—and then he begins
to cry." [4]

> Attention, ladies and gentlemen, your
>   attention please!
> Turn your heads toward this side of the
>   republic for a moment,
> Forget your personal affairs for a night,
> Pleasure and pain can wait at the door:
> A voice is heard from this side of the republic.
> Attention, ladies and gentlemen! your
>   attention please!
>
> A soul that has been bottled up for years
> In a kind of sexual and intellectual abyss,
> Barely feeding himself through the nose
> Wants you to listen to him.
>
> I want to be told about some things,
> I need a little light, the garden is covered with
>   flies,
> I'm in a disastrous mental state,
> I reason in my own way;
> While I say these things I see a bicycle
>   leaning against a wall,
> I see a bridge
> And an automobile that disappears between
>   the buildings.

4. Parra made this comment at a reading of his poetry held at
O'Shea Intermediate School, New York City, in May, 1971. The
reading will be referred to as "O'Shea."

All of you comb your hair, that's true, you walk
   through gardens,
Under your skin you have another skin,
You have a seventh sense
That lets you go in and out automatically,
But I am a child behind the rocks who calls to
   its mother,
I am a pilgrim who kicks stones up to his nose,
A tree that shouts to be covered with leaves.

The opening stanza uses colloquial language for
a public announcement that commands, in bizarre
fashion, a private action: "Forget your personal
affairs for a night." The reader has the sense of lis-
tening to a voice strained by distance, distorted by
the formalistic banality of a loudspeaker, magnified
to the point of incomprehensibility. The ironic pairing
of the public call and the references to "personal
affairs" is emphasized by Parra's use of intimate
forms of address (in Spanish *volved* [turn], *olvidad*
[forget]), and by the phrase "this side of the republic,"
as if the human voice could span the breadth of a
republic.

The mock invocation has more than parodic purposes. Parra makes important figurative statements
in the opening lines. The protagonist evidently feels
an enormous sense of urgency. His plight is of such
consequence that he demands that those who hear
him sacrifice "personal matters" as compelling as
"pleasure" and "pain." He establishes the idea of
distance and isolation, for his call comes from the

other side of the "republic"—over a vast distance that must weaken any voice, even one that is magnified. The repetition of the call for attention, with the addition of exclamation marks, suggests that no one hears his first message, and that the protagonist becomes more and more frantic. Yet despite his frenzied plea and the allusions to the private lives of his presumptive listeners, the protagonist underscores his own isolation by referring to himself in the most impersonal and distant manner possible, as if he were the disembodied voice of an anonymous public official speaking into the microphone of a public address system.

In the second stanza the depersonalized despair of the speaker increases in intensity. He is simply an undifferentiated "voice [that] is heard," "a soul that ... wants you to listen to him." But the people he calls to are now addressed in the formal third person (*ustedes* in Spanish) in contrast to the intimate forms of address used previously. Simultaneously, the protagonist moves from the third to the first person when referring to himself, as if his unheeded call, and the movement away of his supposed listeners (their distance is suggested by the formal mode of address) heightens his frenzied despair so much that he foregoes impersonality and speaks, finally, as himself:

A soul ...
. . . .

Wants you to listen to him.

I want to be told about some things.

The figurative enclosure of the protagonist for a specific period of time is alluded to and developed by means of the phrase "a kind of." It is used in key lines of other poems in the thematic unit, and always refers to the protagonist's imprisonment and faulty perception. In this poem, he is enclosed "In a kind of sexual and intellectual abyss." In "El túnel" his vision is either damanged by "a kind of impenetrable armor" or clouded by "a kind of water vapor." In "Preguntas a la hora del té" he is enveloped in a "kind of mist." Moreover, the "sexual and intellectual abyss" in "El peregrino" has the same enclosing quality that characterizes the imprisonment in the other poems. The "sexual abyss" evokes the malevolent female presence often identified with the trap: his aunts in "El túnel," his mistress in "La víbora," the women around him in "Recuerdos de juventud" and the girl he speaks to on the telephone in "La trampa." In all of these poems sexuality is associated with females who entrap and imprison the male, both psychically and physically. The "intellectual abyss" is an expression of the false attitudes and beliefs which characterize the protagonist's imprisonment. The reference to eating through his nose, for example, suggests a lack of tangible experience which Parra associates with metaphysical and abstract speculations: the only thing that can be "eaten" through the nose is smoke or the aroma of food.[5] The image also prefigures his description of himself at the end of the poem as "a pilgrim who kicks stones up to his nose." The image not only suggests the barren, rocky place of his imprisonment, but also indicates that these stones may be the agony and isolation of his aimless journey, and that therefore the protagonist feeds on his own sorrow. The abyss of his intellectual isolation is evoked in rather laconic but vivid terms:

> I need a little light, the garden is covered
>   with flies,
> I'm in a disastrous mental state,
> I reason in my own way.

Parra's description of the protagonist's abyss is both concrete and indirect. In other words, he calls out only for what he does not have. His requests are concrete, and by extension they define the enclosure. He is in ignorance ("I want to be told about some things"), he is in darkness, in all the literal and figu-

5. The image also brings to mind the allusion to eating in "Notas de viaje" ("I forced myself to eat, I rebelled against myself") and may be linked tangentially to the onion and lettuce that the protagonist notices in "Recuerdos de juventud" and "Notas de viaje" respectively. The vegetables are part of the disconnected, incongruous observations of trivia which are signs of his distraught state, his emotional, physical and intellectual alienation. In this sense too they are comparable to his observation of the bicycle, the bridge and the automobile in this poem.

rative senses of the word ("I need a little light"), and he is rotting, sexually and intellectually ("the garden is covered with flies").[6] He is desolate and alone, while the others are always plural. He is a pilgrim through a rocky landscape while they engage in ordinary, commonplace activities. He is in a desert while they walk through pleasant gardens. He is naked while they are dressed in several skins. He is an abandoned child while the rest seem to possess a special, shared knowledge and understanding from which he is excluded. The protagonist is a child, a pilgrim, a tree; solitary and unprotected he suffers from an intellectual eccentricity that condemns him to an apparently perpetual isolation ("I reason in my own way"). The protagonist's "disastrous mental state"—his "intellectual abyss"—is directly comparable to the artistic introversion described in "El túnel," for both are emblematic of his withdrawal from a society that he peers at through the transparent walls of the bottle-prison or through the distorting prism of his enclosure in the tunnel.

The world outside the prison is presented as the epitome of ordinariness, yet it looks like paradise to

6. Images of plant growth are found in the other poems of the thematic unit and are closely associated with his imprisonment and, on occasion, with the ideas of a failed poetry. Examples of this figure are the agricultural tasks in "El túnel," the forest of chairs and tables in "Recuerdos de juventud," the trees in "Recuerdos de juventud," "El túnel" and "El peregrino," the garden in "La trampa" and "El peregrino," autumn leaves in "Preguntas a la hora del té," "Recuerdos de juventud" and "La víbora."

the protagonist because it seems so strikingly different from his own turmoil. Those "ladies and gentlemen" can engage in any commonplace activity they choose, for they are well protected from the world and from each other. They can walk calmly through gardens that hold no sinister meaning for them, they can comb their hair or pass through a door unthinkingly and feel no impinging menace. They have, in short, the know-how of ordinary living that seems like a magical seventh sense to the protagonist in his isolation. Parra repeats the formal *ustedes* (you) four times in this section of the poem, emphasizing the distance between those on the outside and the persona, and preparing the reader for the emotionally charged ending of the poem. In the final lines the protagonist is described metaphorically, and his extreme separation from the world is stressed, while at the same time Parra reintroduces the possibility of speech as the means of communication with the rest of the world: the child calls, the tree shouts. As if they were contiguous points on the perimeter of a circle, the protagonist's last desperate pleas for help connect with the formalistic and grotesque call for attention that opens the poem. The final images describe the abyss and reiterate and summarize the entire work. The protagonist's side of the republic is a stony place, a bottle-prison that encloses his soul. He calls to the outside, but his language is wrong as it changes from a public announcement to a lost child's cry to the mute shout of a leafless tress. His garden grows nothing but stones, and it is covered with flies, but he can see others strolling through a more fertile landscape. In his despair he can see the outside world, but every effort to reach it is doomed.

"Notas de viaje" specifies the time and localizes the place of the protagonist's solitary imprisonment. The poem intensifies the sense of confinement by counterpointing the protagonist's forced enclosure in a stateroom to the larger enclosure of the ship:

For years I stayed away from my position
I took up traveling, exchanging impressions
   with the people I talked to,
I took up sleeping;
But scenes I had lived through in the past
   would come to mind.
During the dance I would think about absurd
   things:
I would think about some heads of lettuce
   I had seen the day before when I went
   past the kitchen,
I would think no end of fantastic things
   in connection with my family;
Meanwhile the boat had already entered the
   river,
It was making its way through a school of
   jellyfish.
Those photographic scenes affected my mind,
Forced me to shut myself up in my cabin;
I forced myself to eat, I rebelled against
   myself

I constituted a permanent danger on board
Because at any moment I could come out with
    some piece of nonsense.

The ship symbolizes the protagonist's exile, his removal from the world. It also seems to represent an ironic microcosm of a fatuous society whose only noteworthy activities are exchanging impressions and dancing. But Parra also indicates that the sea voyage may be a sign of the protagonist's eventual return to and participation in the world's affairs, for the ship is leaving the high seas, entering the river and presumably coming into port. In other words, the protagonist is returning to his "position"—the useful activity from which he has been separated during his years of wandering imprisonment. The Spanish word *puesto* implies "position" in the sense of a stable emotional center and "occupation" or meaningful work and involvement in social relationships. The protagonist has wilfully abandoned both for the frivolous life on board ship, but he is frustrated in his attempts to participate in it. He is plagued by obsessive rumination about the most irrelevant matters and tormented by acute observations of minutiae which disturb his misdirected efforts at communication. In "El peregrino," for example, the protagonist is distracted by a bicycle, a bridge, an automobile and buildings at the very moment that he calls out to those who move freely through the world. In "Notas de viaje" the trivia of ordinary living again interpose themselves between him and the world he tries to reach; he remembers some heads of lettuce as he attempts to take part in a commonplace social activity like dancing.

The protagonist's thoughts and actions on the ship are consistently inane. He is driven mad by "scenes" —his past experiences—tries to contain his frenzy by thinking about lettuce and finally has to retreat into his cabin—an act which is tantamount to doubling the enclosure around him. But the ship and its passengers are equally absurd. They represent no real options to the imprisonment, and are as insignificant and unimportant as the travels, conversations, and sleep that replace his "position." In a very real sense they *are* his imprisonment, his withdrawal from his proper position in the world. The desperate protagonist strains to communicate with a world that is simply not worth the effort.

Sexuality is a prominent component of the protagonist's enclosure. In "El peregrino" Parra describes the abyss as both sexual and intellectual; the dance in "Notas de viaje" is a sign of eroticism which is expanded in "La víbora" into a symbol of frenzied desire. In "Notas de viaje" the distractions which plague the protagonist while he is dancing evoke the sexual alienation which is an integral part of his social isolation, and the incident which triggers his hysterical withdrawal into his stateroom—and which, ironically, indicates the passage home—is the difficult passage of the ship through a "school of jellyfish." The reference is similar to the sexual allusion "kind of jelly" in "Recuerdos de juventud" and suggests the female genitals. In other words, Parra represents women and sexuality as both the way into and the way out of the enclosing prison. And although it is intercourse itself that imprisons and encloses the protagonist, Parra also describes women, somewhat sardonically, as the salvation of the human race in "Los vicios del mundo moderno" (The Vices of the Modern World):

> Let us try to be happy, that's what I
>   recommend, by sucking at the miserable
>   human rib.
> Let us draw from it the restorative fluid,
> . . . .
> Let us cling to this divine bit of flesh!
> Let us suck at these lips that drive us mad;
> Let us breathe this enervating and
>   destructive perfume
> And live the life of the elect for one more
>   day.
> Man gets the wax he needs to shape the faces
>   of his idols from under his armpits.
> And from women's sex the straw and mud
>   for his temples.

But the promise of the return in "Notas de viaje" is unfulfilled. The ship never actually reaches port, and the protagonist is not yet free.

"La trampa" explores the two distinct but intimately related manifestations of the protagonist's

imprisonment. This is a poem about the "sexual
and intellectual abyss":

> During that time I would flee scenes that were
>   too mysterious.
> Like people with stomach trouble who avoid
>   heavy meals,
> I preferred to stay at home elucidating
>   certain questions
> Concerning the reproduction of spiders,
> To which end I would shut myself up
>   in the garden
> And not appear in public until the early hours
>   of the morning;
> Or in shirtsleeves, in a defiant attitude,
> I would also hurl angry glances at the moon
> Trying to avoid those evil-tempered thoughts
> That stick to the human soul like polyps.
> When I was alone I had absolute control
>   over myself,
> I would go back and forth fully conscious of
>   my actions
> Or stretch out among the boards in the cellar
> And dream, and think up procedures, and
>   resolve minor emergencies.
> Those were the times when I put my famous
>   oneiric method into operation,
> Which consists of doing violence to yourself,
>   and dreaming whatever you want,
> And instigating scenes arranged beforehand
>   with the help of the Beyond.

In this way I managed to obtain valuable data
Concerning a whole series of doubts that afflict
    our lives:
Trips abroad, erotic confusions, religious
    complexes.
But all my precautions were useless
Because for reasons that are hard to explain
I began to slide automatically down a kind of
    inclined plane,
Like a balloon losing air my soul lost altitude,
My instinct for self-preservation stopped
    working
And deprived of my most essential prejudices
I fell fatally into the trap of the telephone
That attracts everything around it, like an
    abyss,
And with trembling hands I dialed that
    damned number
That I still repeat automatically while I'm
    sleeping.
Those moments were filled with uncertainty
    and misery
While I, like a skeleton standing in front of
    that infernal table
Covered with yellow cretonne,
Waited for an answer from the other end of
    the world,
The other half of myself a prisoner in a pit.
Those intermittent noises on the telephone
Affected me like a dentist's drill,
They sank into my soul like needles thrown
    down from above

Until, when the moment finally arrived,
I began to perspire and to stammer
    feverishly.
My tongue was like a piece of veal
Hanging between me and the girl I was
    talking to
Like those black curtains that separate us
    from the dead.
I didn't want to have those conversations that
    were too intimate
But I provoked them anyway, like a fool,
With my voice full of desire, charged with
    electricity.
When I heard myself called by my first name
In that tone of forced intimacy
I was filled with vague discomfort,
With agonizing localized disturbances that I
    tried to ward off
By means of a system of rapid questions
    and answers
That created a state of pseudoerotic
    excitation in her
And that eventually affected me as well
Taking the form of incipient erections and a
    feeling of failure
Then I'd force myself to laugh and then I'd
    fall into a state of mental prostration.
Those absurd conversations would go on
    for hours
Until the landlady of the boarding house
    appeared behind the screen
And brusquely interrupted that stupid idyll,

Those contortions of a candidate for heaven
And those catastrophes that were so
   depressing to my spirit
But which did not stop completely when I
   hung up the phone
Since, generally, we would have a date
To see each other the next day at a soda
   fountain
Or in the door of a church whose name I don't
   care to remember.

During "that time," the specific period of imprisonment mentioned in so many of the poems of the
thematic unit, the protagonist avoids "scenes that
were too mysterious" by fleeing into his emotional
imprisonment and withdrawal. The opening of the
poem establishes the important rhetorical figure of
flight by referring to his enclosure in the house and in
the garden, where the protagonist sets up protective
barriers between himself and a menacing reality that
is represented by the mysterious "scenes." Inside the
enclosure he devotes himself to that strangely com-
pulsive cerebration which characterizes the intellectual abyss. His fruitless meditations, sometimes
metaphysical, sometimes trivial, are associated with
the garden—that is, with the figure of plant growth
that is a constant sign of the imprisonment. His other
activities, too, are maniacally insignificant. Parra's
description is ironic in the extreme as he presents the
protagonist hurling "angry glances at the moon" or
lying down in the cellar to solve "minor emergencies."

The protagonist's useless anger with the cosmos and his solitary cerebration introduce the burlesque of the "famous oneiric method," reminiscent of his "automatic writing" and "spiritualist conception of the world" in "El túnel"; in both poems these actions and attitudes are meant to signify flight and withdrawal into a devastating intellectual isolation. The "valuable data" he obtains inside the enclosure is in fact valueless because it is the result of avoiding "evil-tempered thoughts" and "scenes that were too mysterious." In short, he spends his days and nights in a frenzy of busy activity that is insignificant and unquestionably foolish. His preoccupation with the distractions inside the enclosure are rather like the efforts of the squirrel to keep the wheel inside his cage turning. Similarly, the protagonist's meaningless but absorbing projects are part of his frantic attempt to maintain his precarious emotional balance on the edge of the precipice. But his "precautions," his "instinct for self-preservation" and his "prejudices" all fail him, and he falls into the abyss of frustrated and ungratified sexuality, represented by the telephone because it is a mechanical and secondhand means of communication. Parra complicates the imagery by presenting the intellectual abyss as the protagonist's enclosure and withdrawal into the house and garden, and then by representing the sexual abyss in the concrete physical image of the protagonist sliding down the sides of a chasm.

The poem is actually divided into two sections. The first describes the intellectual disasters that the protagonist falls victim to, while the second elaborates his grotesque and stifled sexuality. It is not by accident that his tortured eroticism as he slides into the abyss of frustrated sexuality is conceived of as the fall, for the perversions of love that await the protagonist at the bottom of the pit are indeed the primal and original sin. Nevertheless, the intellectual abyss at the brink of the sexual one has an equally shattering effect on him. If in the first he avoids contact with the real world by withdrawing and enclosing himself, in the second he avoids the physical enclosure of the sexual embrace by using the telephone as his means of communication, by indulging in false, unsatisfying stimulation, by meeting the woman in public places. Significantly, Parra introduces a new set of images based on sickness and death, and relates them directly to the sexual imagery and the trope of enclosure and imprisonment. The rhetorical figure of sickness is manifest in the semiscientific jargon used in this section of the poem, and in the protagonist's descriptions of his terrible mental and physical anguish. They appear in the following order:

my soul lost altitude

with trembling hands I dialed that damned
   number

Those moments were filled with uncertainty
   and misery

Those intermittent noises on the telephone
Affected me like a dentist's drill,
They sank into my soul like needles
. . . .
I began to perspire and to stammer feverishly.

I was filled with vague discomfort,
With agonizing localized disturbances . . .

. . . a state of pseudoerotic excitation
. . . that eventually affected me as well
Taking the form of incipient erections
    and a feeling of failure.
Then I'd force myself to laugh and then I'd
    fall into a state of mental prostration.

The images of death include the failure of the protagonist's "instinct for self-preservation" which is
responsible for his falling "fatally" into the abyss, the
protagonist's comparison of himself to a "skeleton" in
front of an "infernal" telephone table, and his stut-
tering conversation which he compares to the "black
curtains that separate us from the dead." The association of sexuality with death, disease and emotional malaise transforms the primary image of enclosure and imprisonment into a malevolent female
metaphor. For the protagonist, sexuality itself is the
trap and the most despesperate expression of his
alienation.
    Parra renders the protagonist's disordered, tor-

mented state by alternating the grotesque sobriety of semimedical terminology ("localized disturbances," "pseudoerotic excitation," "incipient erections") with prosaic, commonplace objects and words ("yellow cretonne," "veal steak," "soda fountain") and evocations of sexual frustration that are closely related to the disease imagery ("vague discomforts," "a feeling of failure," "catastrophes that were so depressing to my spirit"). These indications of physical and emotional disturbance are an ironic contrast to the protagonist's feigned self-reliance and control which are described in the first section of the poem. His alleged dominion of himself is clearly an illusion based on the fact that he poses trivial questions, responds with false answers, and lives the withdrawn, isolated life which is equivalent to the intellectual abyss.

At the end of "La trampa" Parra adds a literary dimension to his exploration of the abyss that entraps the protagonist. The final words, "whose name I don't care to remember," are quoted directly from the opening sentence of *Don Quixote* ("In a village of La Mancha whose name I don't care to remember ...."). Both Don Quixote and the antipoetic protagonist suffer from illusions which sometimes border on lunacy. The Cervantine reference suggests that the poem is a burlesque of traditional courtship, echoing Cervantes' parody of chivalry. The protagonist's rarified intellectualism and painful avoidance of consummation are contemporary versions of the courteous tradition. Both the ancient courtly ideal of *amour courteois* and the modern telephone are tan-

tamount to eroticism at a distance, and to Parra's
mind they constitute the sexual abyss.

"Recuerdos de juventud" presents most of the
major motifs of the thematic unit, expanding the
imagery, using associative references and quoting
directly from the other poems. Parra has called the
theme of the poem "a youthful inability to
communicate," [7] and in this relatively short work he
concentrates the details of the protagonist's literary
isolation, his sexual frustration, aimless wandering
and his unsuccessful efforts to break out of the prison:

> What's certain is that I kept going back and
>   forth,
> Sometimes I bumped into trees,
> I bumped into beggars,
> I would make my way through a forest of
>   chairs and tables,
> With my soul hanging by a thread I would
>   watch the great leaves fall.
> But all of it was useless,
> I kept sinking deeper and deeper into a kind
>   of jelly;
> People would laugh at my fits of rage,
> Individuals would shake in their armchairs like
>   algae moved by the waves
> And women gave me hate-filled looks
> Making me cry and laugh against my will.

7. He made these remarks to Homero Aridjis.

All of this produced a feeling of disgust,
It produced a storm of incoherent sentences,
Threats, insults, oaths that were beside the
    point,
It produced certain exhausting hip movements,
Those funereal dances
That left me breathless
And unable to lift my head for days
And nights on end.

I kept going back and forth, it's true,
My soul floated down the streets
Asking for help, asking for a little tenderness;
With a sheet of paper and a pencil I would go
    into cemeteries
Determined not to let them fool me.
I would go round and round the same subject,
I would observe things closely
Or in a fit of fury I would tear out my hair.

That's how I made my debut in the classrooms,
 Like a man with a gunshot wound I dragged
    myself through the literary societies,
I crossed the thresholds of private houses,
With the sharp edge of my tongue I tried to
    communicate with the spectators:
They would read their newspapers
Or disappear behind a taxi.
Then where could I go!
By that time the store was closed;

I would think about a slice of onion that I
   saw at supper
And about the abyss that separates us
   from the other abysses.

The poems of the thematic unit establish direct con-
nections among the abyss and women, marine
images, plant growth and physical disease. These
aspects of the imprisonment are extended and
emphasized in "Recuerdos de juventud." In the first
section Parra gives the details of the protagonist's
involuntary fall into the abyss, underscoring the confusion and uncertainty which characterize the imprisonment by beginning the poem *in media res*. The
opening phrase "What's certain" implies that the
next statement is the only sure, fixed fact that
the protagonist can hold on to, and the certainty is
only that he "kept going back and forth." These
same words also express the protagonist's aimless
wandering in "La trampa" ("I would go back and
forth fully conscious of my actions").

In "Recuerdos de juventud" the artifacts of daily
life, merely observed in the other poems of the
thematic unit, become menacing obstacles which ob-
struct the protagonist's path as he moves "back and
forth." These commonplace objects are identified
with plant growth in the image "a forest of tables
and chairs," and consequently, they take on the
qualities of malevolence attributed to gardens and
forests in the other poems. At the same time, because

of comparable wording, the line "I would make my way through a forest of chairs and tables" is related to ". . . the ship . . ./Made its way through a school of jellyfish" in "Notas de viaje." This similarity suggests a secondary identification of the images of plant growth with those of the sea, and emphasizes that both are obstacles in the protagonist's path. Moreover, the series of marine references—the verb "sinking," the use of the word "jelly" (cf. "jellyfish"), and the simile "Individuals would shake in their armchairs like algae moved by the waves"—contributes to the association of the two sets of images and reinforces the rhetorical figure of the abyss with which they are both identified.

The protagonist describes his desperate situation by stating that "all of it was useless." The phrase duplicates the line "All my precautions were useless" in "La trampa," and in both poems the protagonist envisions his anguish in the same terms: he loses his footing and falls into the sexual abyss. In "La trampa" he slides "down a kind of inclined plane," and in "Recuerdos de juventud" he sinks into "a kind of jelly," where "women would give me hate-filled looks/Making me go up, making me go down/Making me cry and laugh against my will." The unambiguous connotations of these lines complete the constant association of sexuality with the imprisonment; he is the victim of women insofar as they are sexual beings, and very much their puppet. His soul and body are helpless in their scornful hands, and they toy with him as he hangs "by a thread." The protagonist shows all the signs of sexual desire, but his sensations are depicted as painful and involuntary. Women, who stimulate his desire, hate him. In all probability this only reflects his hatred for them, for women are the reason he feels "vague discomfort," "agonizing localized disturbances" and "incipient erections" in "La trampa." In "Recuerdos de juventud" his symptoms are intensified, emphasizing the protagonist's identification of eroticism with disease and death and his deep hatred and fear of sexuality and everything connected with it:

All of this produced a feeling of disgust,
. . . .
It produced certain exhausting hip movements,
Those funereal dances
That left me breathless
And unable to lift my head for days
And nights on end.

The protagonist is so alienated from other people that even the sexual embrace is envisioned as enclosure in an imprisoning abyss. At the same time his thought processes are reduced to "fits of rage" ("Recuerdos de juventud"), or a "state of mental prostration" and careful inquiries into the "reproduction of spiders" ("La trampa"), or the "practice of automatic writing" ("El túnel"). He is invariably considered absurd by those who surround him but refuse to have any relation with him, and his frantic, mindless busyness leads only to greater anguish and despair.

In the first section of the poem Parra describes the prison. In the second, he depicts the protagonist's abortive, failed efforts to leave the prison and participate in the human relationships of the real world. In a variation of the phrase that begins the poem, Parra reemphasizes the aimless wandering and confusion which torment his pathetic antihero ("I kept going back and forth, it's true"). The protagonist tries to clarify and understand his situation, but the only truth that he can recognize is that he does indeed wander aimlessly through his alienation, his enclosure. This is vividly presented in the image of the protagonist's soul afloat in the streets. Its movements are involuntary, and it is separated from the solid ground of the physical world. Parra's reintroduction of marine imagery underscores the helpless terrors of the enclosed, alienated life that the protagonist leads, for the sea is consistently identified with the imprisonment—as are the images of plant growth, for example—and in this poem its negative qualities even affect those outside the enclosure ("Individuals would shake in their armchairs like algae moved by the waves"). At the mercy of forces he can neither define nor overcome, the protagonist goes through the streets asking for help and tenderness. He is actually pleading for relation, for connection with people, as he does in "El peregrino." His struggle for personal contact is linked to literary efforts which should be a form of profound communication with the world, but which, like "automatic writing," only fortify and strengthen the imprisonment. His writing, like his frustrated sexuality, is associated with death; love and poetry, potentially the deepest communion with others, are only another manifestation of alienation and imprisonment during the protagonist's period of isolation. They are his "sexual and intellectual abyss." Therefore, the references to writing—his visits to the cemetery—are desperately melancholy. He turns round and round, indulges in his idiosyncratic scrutiny of minutiae and is subject to meaningless fits of rage. Keeping in mind the avant-garde writing techniques which are emblems of the imprisonment in "El túnel," Parra's description of this aspect of the "intellectual abyss" is probably aimed at the poets of the coterie—poets who are removed and isolated and whose work is abstruse, opaque and rarified. Whether Parra is recalling the period before he became the antipoet is a problematical question, but the protagonist's literary activities are clearly and intimately related to his intellecutal alienation. In the classroom, in private houses, in literary societies he suffers and is alone. Those he encounters are not students or colleagues but spectators, nonparticipants who engage in the ordinary, trivial actions characteristic of the world outside the prison. Like their counterparts in "El peregrino" whom he observes and calls to while they comb their hair and stroll through gardens, the people in "Recuerdos de juventud" read newspapers or hurriedly walk away from him. Their refusal to allow direct contact leads

inevitably to the ironic conclusion of the poem with its
abrasive juxtaposition of the ludicrous and the
dreadful:

> Then where could I go!
> By that time the store was closed;
> I would think about a slice of onion that I saw
>   at supper
> And about the abyss that separates us from
>   the other abysses.

After one of his typically inane observations, the
protagonist realizes that his self and his abyss have
become inseparable definitions of one another. The
onion, like the lettuce in "Notas de viaje," is a sign of
his deranged condition. At the same time, his observations of the onion and the lettuce are a pathetic
indication of the protagonist's efforts to maintain
some connection—any connection—with concrete
reality. His life, like the lives of those who surround
him (even though they appear to possess the ability to
maneuver their way through the trivial details of
daily existence) is defined by suffering. Despite the
protagonist's acknowledgment of shared anguish—
perhaps the first step toward freedom—he still sees an
unbridgeable chasm between his "abyss" (his self)
and all the other abysses. This gulf of isolation is
identical with his sexual and intellectual alienation.
Ironically, his impasse is symbolized as a closed store
(he is locked out instead of being locked in) and the
equation of onions and abysses is emblematic of his

disjointed, distracted thought processes and his intolerable emotional state.

The terrible, victimizing females of the protagonist's imprisonment are personified and summarized in "La víbora." [8] Leaving behind the inane frustrations, the "stupid idyll" of "La trampa," the tedious agricultural chores of "El túnel," in this poem he is utterly seduced and caught in the viper's jellied trap of sexual domination and exploitation, senseless activity and petty crime. "La víbora" explores the worst aspects of the "sexual and intellectual abyss," and yet it is the only poem of the thematic unit that promises escape from the enclosure. The protagonist, from the depths of his lack of will, finally demands something real, something necessary and something concrete and makes the first important move toward union with the tangible, social world which is, for Parra, the sign of emancipation:

For many long years I was condemned to love
   a contemptible woman
To sacrifice myself for her, to suffer
   countless humiliations and deceptions,
To work day and night to feed and clothe her,

8. Parra's comments on this poem are strangely contradictory. At O'Shea he said that it refers to "no real person," and categorically denied any connection between the figure of the viper and his first wife. However, he told Homero Aridjis that the poem is relatively autobiographical and describes his first marriage.

To carry out a few crimes, commit a few
    misdeameanors,
Perform petty burglaries by the light of
    the moon,
Forgeries of compromising documents,
For fear of being disgraced in the sight
    of her fascinating eyes.
When we got along we would meet in parks
And have our picture taken together
    steering a motorboat,
Or we would go to a nightclub
Where we would lose ourselves in
    shameless dancing
That went on until all hours of the morning.
For long years I lived a prisoner under the
    spell of that woman
Who would show up in my office completely
    naked
Performing unimaginable contortions
Intended to draw my poor soul into her orbit
And, above all, to get hold of my last cent.
She gave me strict orders not to have anything
    to do with my family.
My friends were alienated from me by means
    of defamatory libels
That the viper had published in a newspaper
    that she owned.
Deliriously passionate, she didn't give me a
    minute's peace,
Urgently demanding that I kiss her mouth
And immediately answer her foolish questions

Several of which had to do with eternity and
   the afterlife,
Subjects which made me feel terrible
And gave me buzzing in the ears, recurrent
   nausea, sudden fainting spells
That she knew how to take advantage of with
   that spirit of practicality that was
   characteristic of her—
She would put on her clothes without wasting
   any time
And leave my apartment and me in the lurch.

This situation lasted for more than five years.
Sometimes we would live together, sharing
   the rent,
In a round room in a high class neighborhood
   near the cemetery.
(Some nights we had to interrupt our
   honeymoon
And fight off the rats that squeezed
   in through the window).

The viper kept a detailed account book
Where she wrote down every penny I
   borrowed from her;
She didn't even let me use her toothbrush
   although I had given it to her myself
And she accused me of having ruined her youth:
With flashing eyes she subpoenaed me to
   appear in court

And pay part of what I owed her with all due
    speed
Because she needed that money to continue
    her studies.
Then I had to take to the street and live on
    public charity,
Sleeping on the benches in the square
Where the police often found me half dead
Among the first autumn leaves.
Fortunately that situation did not go on
    much longer
Because once when I was in a square again
Posing to have my picture taken
A pair of delicious feminine hands suddenly
    covered my eyes
While a voice that I loved asked guess-who.
You're my love, I answered calmly
Darling! she said nervously.
Let me sit on your knees one more time!
Then I could see that she now came complete
    with a small loincloth.
It was a memorable meeting, though full of
    discordant notes:
I've bought some land, not far from the
    slaughterhouse, she exclaimed,
I plan to build a kind of pyramid there
Where we can spend the rest of our lives.
I've finished my studies, I've passed the bar
    exam,
I'm pretty well off;

Let's go into some profitable business, just the
   two of us, my love, she added,
Let's build our nest far from the world.
That's enough nonsense, I answered, your
   plans make me suspicious,
Remember that at any time my real wife
Could leave us all in the most frightful poverty.
My children are grown up now, time has
   gone by,
I'm absolutely exhausted, let me rest for a
   minute,
Woman, bring me a little water,
Get me something to eat somewhere,
I'm dying of hunger,
I can't work for you anymore,
Everything is finished between us.

The poem describes the sexual abyss. Typically, the
protagonist sees himself as both the prisoner and the
victim of a woman whom he calls a viper with "fas-
cinating eyes." Parra suggests the traditional belief
that snakes have the power to hypnotize their victims
and draw them near against their will, just as the
protagonist is attracted and seduced by women into
his involuntary prison. His life in the trap is filled
with meaningless activity and trivia, but under the
sexual spell of the viper he even commits crimes.

During the period of his imprisonment they visit
parks and pose for photographs in motorboats. These
references recall the plant and marine imagery which

are primary signs of the abyss. The viper and her victim also engage in an erotic dance which is the first of a series of carnal allusions which move the poem onto a plane of bizarre, comic fantasy:

> ... that woman
> ... would appear in my office completely
>   naked
> Performing unimaginable contortions

The sexual ambience in the poem becomes grotesque, while at the same time the figurative language used to evoke the woman undergoes a subtle change. More vampire than serpent, she is intent upon sucking out his soul—his very life—with her incessant, peremptory demands upon his mind and body:

> Deliriously passionate, she didn't give me a
>   minute's peace,
> Urgently demanding that I kiss her mouth
> And immediately answer her foolish
>   questions
> Several of which had to do with eternity and
>   the afterlife

Her metaphysical questions, echoes of the protagonist's own "spiritualist conception of the world" in "El túnel," are a passing reference to the intellectual abyss, but the viper's connection to the protagonist is mainly one of control through sexual domination. Parodically, Parra denies her the malevolent glamor of the great temptresses: she is no Lilith, no Delilah, but merely a greedy, exploitative opportunist, a physically attractive version of the grasping aunts in "El túnel."

For the protagonist, sexuality means a demented life, subjugation to involuntary desires, seduction and domination by women. Small wonder, then, that eroticism and images of disease are again associated with one another: in this sexual abyss he feels "terrible," and suffers from "buzzing in the ears, recurrent nausea, sudden fainting spells." His ghoulish liaison with the viper—that is, his imprisonment—goes on for five years. Part of the time is spent in a round room, one of the most charged and revealing references in the poem. It is associated with their awful sexuality, ironically called a "honeymoon," and with the viper's greed which is symbolized by her "account book," her careful guarding of her toothbrush and the subpoena she serves on the protagonist. The description of their life together is a serious parody that is based on grotesque exaggerations and ironic disparities between symbols and their referents. The accumulated absurdities and incongruous trivia are as shockingly comic as a surrealistic dream sequence. The rats, for example, and the cemetery, the subpoena and the account book are emblematic of the protagonist's tortured life in the sexual abyss. The most important image of imprisonment, however, is the round room itself, which represents enclosure in straightforwardly sexual, female terms. It is a clear sign of love debased, of the sexual abyss and of the terrible isolation that results from the experience of sexuality as a never-ending imprisonment.

The imprisonment is terminated twice. In the first instance their separation, initiated not entirely of the protagonist's own free will, leads to the humiliating circumstance of his living on "public charity." Significantly, his initial attempt to free himself from the domination of the viper is associated with the image of plant growth: the "first leaves of autumn" recall the "great leaves" in "Recuerdos de juventud" and the "dry leaves" in "Preguntas a la hora del té." The plant imagery, consistently identified with the protagonist's alienation and enclosure, indicates that he is still imprisoned despite his break with the viper. Trapped in his own aimlessness and propensity for leaving himself to the mercy of others, he is a desperately isolated figure. His self-liberating gesture is doomed to failure; he does not yet understand freedom.

His second attempt at escape is described in the closing lines of the poem, a whirlwind of fantastic images mixed with laughably mundane details. In the final section Parra wears the mask of the trivial, the prosaic and the comic that marks his moments of greatest intensity and is the sign of the antipoetic synthesis. He describes the protagonist posing for a photograph, and then has the viper return unexpectedly, dressed in a loincloth and coyly playing "guess-who" with her former victim. This concatenation of incongruities is the ultimate parody of the protagonist's life with her, for certain elements are

THE TECHNIQUE OF ANTIPOETRY   153

reiterated here that appear in the first section of the poem. They used to pose for photographs together, the viper's appearance in a loincloth in a public square repeats her naked invasions of his office, and her desire to sit in his lap suggests her "unimaginable contortions." Their meeting is indeed "memorable, although full of discordant notes." Even the viper's efforts to lure him back—a simple task, apparently, since he still thinks of her as his "love"—are a sardonic burlesque. The image of the viper dressed in a loincloth and trying to sit in the protagonist's unwilling lap is followed by her imbecilic temptation of a profitable little business-cum-love nest far from worldly cares. But behind the parodic façade are the inescapable emotional realities of her efforts to seduce him back into the prison. Her eroticism is still venal and deadly: the love nest would be a pyramid,[9] the altar of the sacrificial victim and the monument to death, near the slaughterhouse (cf. the cemetery near the round room) but far from the world, although the protagonist's major problem is how to get back into the world. The viper offers him more of the same, but worse, and the protagonist rejects her proposition with a masterfully comic bit of understatement ("your plans make me suspicious"). He turns to his own pressing material needs and refuses to be caught by her again. And here lies his hope, but a hope made

9. The phrase "a kind of," used in the other poems in connection with the imprisonment, indicates that accepting her offer would be tantamount to reentering the enclosure.

melancholy by his mental and physical exhaustion. He definitively rejects the life she offers, not with the brusque youthful return to reality of "El túnel," but with the tired gesture of an old and disillusioned man who still depends on his worst enemy for sustenance.

In the poems of the thematic unit the trope of enclosure—the fact of the protagonist's isolation—is causally related to his refusal or inability to take the action necessary for self-liberation. He actually chooses his prison and the inane activities with which he fills his days. His tormented relations with the rest of the world are the result of his incapacity to confront reality without some intervening, protective barrier that symbolically represents the walls of his prison, the sides of the sexual and intellectual abyss. The barrier invariably prevents the persona from making emotional contact with other people. It is presented in several ways: as distracted thought and speech at moments of critical emotional tension, as ignoble failures in literature and philosophy, as sexuality which is experienced as joyless victimization, and as vapid, meaningless activity. These manifestations of crippled emotional life and their concomitant symptoms of physical disease are presented in a series of ironic signals that trigger the reader's contemptuous amusement despite the protagonist's pathetic suffering. They form a dissonant background to the motif of these poems—the theme of tormented consciousness—for they provoke a scornful response to the protagonist's plight.

These ironic signals consist of the extremely banal objects and actions which evoke the imprisonment, the prosaic language that the protagonist uses to describe his suffering (clichés, inane understatements or jargon), and the inept, evasive rationalizations which he offers in self-justification. Because of their essentially comic quality, all of the ironic signals are violently incongruous with the protagonist's despair, laying the foundation for the feeling of distance between the observer and the persona. This antipoetic synthesis of inconsistent sign systems (the ironic signals on the one hand, the protagonist's despair on the other) leads the reader to feel his own superiority to the protagonist's bungling ineptitude and clichéd expression. Parra emphasizes and ridicules the persona's pathetic circumstance by stressing the comic, absurd potential in even the most pitiable feelings and situations. Then, too, we seem to perceive the protagonist's emotional dilemma more clearly than he does himself. He allows himself to be trapped by obvious enemies, he permits their cruel exploitation of his mental, emotional and physical energies and he contributes to his misery with dissimulation and cowardice. In effect, he sanctions the existence of the prison and permits it to continue for years. But the reader sees himself as too clever and too insightful to be so deceived and victimized. Our sense of psychic distance from the protagonist evolves from our initial perception of the absurdities inherent in the poetic situation, and this same ironic distance accounts for the strong comic impact of the poems.

On reflection, however, the observer's feeling of superiority fades when we perceive a community of experience with the persona that is based on the profound human significance of his condition and on our recognition of that condition as our own. We too have been duped and seduced. We have been desperately uncertain, and have not known how to communicate our despair, or to whom. We too have accepted untenable situations as inevitable or inescapable for the sake of not facing the awful dangers of the unknown. We have deceived ourselves and others for the sake of emotional survival and found ourselves incoherent and distracted at crucial moments. We too have feigned talents and capacities when confronted by an apparently universal special knowledge from which we had been mysteriously excluded, deliberately provoked harmful actions and situations, called out and shouted and not been heard. In short, we too have been imprisoned in our incapacity for freedom.

This realization of the ultimate identity of reader and persona profoundly affects the structure of the poems. Our involvement with the protagonist necessarily changes our perception of the poetic statement; the irony boomerangs and flies directly toward us, for if the signs of the protagonist's isolation are failed efforts to express sexuality, artistic and intellectual obscurity, a belief in the reality of metaphysical problems and the inability to save himself from inwardly and outwardly imposed imprisonments, then regardless of clichés, jargon and trivia, his alienation is no comic matter, and we are obliged to ask which of our attitudes or postures confront the world more adequately. The despair and the foolishness of this protagonist are our own. We are he, and he is Everyman.

Parra forces the identification of protagonist and reader, and then incorporates the reader's changing perceptions and responses into the very ambience and structure of each poem. Parra's antipoetic synthesis joins the disparate elements in each work into a single vision of a mortifying human condition. In the world of antipoetry absurdity, pathos, rage, frustration and despair are an ineluctable inheritance from which no one, not even the reader, can escape.

Appendix

Advertencia
al
lector

El autor no responde de las molestias que puedan
  ocasionar sus escritos
Aunque le pese
El lector tendrá que darse siempre por satisfecho.
Sabelius, que además de teólogo fue un humorista
  consumado,
Después de haber reducido a polvo el dogma de la
  Santísima Trinidad
¿Respondió acaso de su herejía?
Y si llegó a responder, ¡cómo lo hizo!
¡En qué forma descabellada!
¡Basándose en qué cúmulo de contradicciones!

Según los doctores de la ley este libro no debiera
  publicarse:
La palabra arco iris no aparece en él en ninguna parte,

Menos aún la palabra dolor,
La palabra torcuato.
Sillas y mesas sí que figuran a granel.
¡Ataúdes!, ¡útiles de escritorio!
Lo que me llena de orgullo
Porque, a mi modo de ver, el cielo se está cayendo a
   pedazos.

Los mortales que hayan leído el Tractatus de
   Wittgenstein
Pueden darse con una piedra en el pecho
Porque es una obra difícil de conseguir:
Pero el Círculo de Viena se disolvió hace años,
Sus miembros se dispersaron sin dejar huella
Y yo he decidido declarar la guerra a los cavalieri della
   luna.

Mi poesía puede perfectamente no conducir a nin-
   guna parte:
"¡Las risas de este libro son falsas!", argumentarán
   mis detractores
"Sus lágrimas, ¡artificiales!"
"En vez de suspirar, en estas páginas se bosteza"
"Se patalea como un niño de pecho"
"El autor se da a entender a estornudos"
Conforme: os invito a quemar vuestras naves,
Como los fenicios pretendo formarme mi propio
   alfabeto.
"¿A qué molestar al público entonces?", se pregunt-
   arán los amigos lectores:

"Si el propio autor empieza por desprestigiar sus
  escritos,
¡Qué podrá esperarse de ellos!"
Cuidado, yo no desprestigio nada
O, mejor dicho, yo exalto mi punto de vista,
Me vanaglorio de mis limitaciones
Pongo por las nubes mis creaciones.

Los pájaros de Aristófanes
Enterraban en sus propias cabezas
Los cadáveres de sus padres.
(Cada pájaro era un verdadero cementerio volante)
A mi modo de ver
Ha llegado la hora de modernizar esta ceremonia
¡Y yo entierro mis plumas en la cabeza de los señores
  lectores!

Cambios
de
nombre

A los amantes de las bellas letras
Hago llegar mis mejores deseos
Voy a cambiar de nombre a algunas cosas.

Mi posición es ésta:
El poeta no cumple su palabra
Si no cambia los nombres de las cosas.

¿Con qué razón el sol
Ha de seguir llamándose sol?
¡Pido que se le llame Micifuz
El de las botas de cuarenta leguas!

¿Mis zapatos parecen ataúdes?
Sepan que desde hoy en adelante
Los zapatos se llaman ataúdes.

162

Comuníquese, anótese y publíquese
Que los zapatos han cambiado de nombre:
Desde ahora se llaman ataúdes.

Bueno, la noche es larga
Todo poeta que se estime a sí mismo
Debe tener su propio diccionario
Y antes que se me olvide
Al propio dios hay que cambiarle nombre
Que cada cual lo llame como quiera:
Ese es un problema personal.

Manifiesto

Señoras y señores
Esta es nuestra última palabra.
—Nuestra primera y última palabra—
Los poetas bajaron del Olimpo.

Para nuestros mayores
La poesía fue un objeto de lujo
Pero para nosotros
Es un artículo de primera necesidad:
No podemos vivir sin poesía.

A diferencia de nuestros mayores
—Y esto lo digo con todo respeto—
Nosotros sostenemos
Que el poeta no es un alquimista
El poeta es un hombre como todos

Un albañil que construye su muro:
Un constructor de puertas y ventanas.

Nosotros conversamos
En el lenguaje de todos los días
No creemos en signos cabalísticos.

Además una cosa:
El poeta está ahí
Para que el árbol no crezca torcido.

Este es nuestro mensaje.
Nosotros denunciamos al poeta demiurgo
Al poeta Barata
Al poeta Ratón de Biblioteca.
Todos estos señores
—Y esto lo digo con mucho respeto—
Deben ser procesados y juzgados
Por construir castillos en el aire
Por malgastar el espacio y el tiempo
Redactando sonetos a la luna
Por agrupar palabras al azar
A la última moda de París.
Para nosotros no:
El pensamiento no nace en la boca
Nace en el corazón del corazón.

Nosotros repudiamos
La poesía de gafas obscuras
La poesía de capa y espada
La poesía de sombrero alón.

Propiciamos en cambio
La poesía a ojo desnudo
La poesía a pecho descubierto
La poesía a cabeza desnuda.

No creemos en ninfas ni tritones.
La poesía tiene que ser esto:
Una muchacha rodeada de espigas
O no ser absolutamente nada.

Ahora bien, en el plano político
Ellos, nuestros abuelos inmediatos,
¡Nuestros buenos abuelos inmediatos!
Se refractaron y se dispersaron
Al pasar por el prisma de cristal.
Unos pocos se hicieron comunistas.
Yo no sé si lo fueron realmente.
Supongamos que fueron comunistas,
Lo que sé es una cosa:
Que no fueron poetas populares,
Fueron unos reverendos poetas burgueses.

Hay que decir las cosas como son:
Sólo uno que otro
Supo llegar al corazón del pueblo.
Cada vez que pudieron
Se declararon de palabra y de hecho
Contra la poesía dirigida
Contra la poesía del presente
Contra la poesía proletaria.

Aceptemos que fueron comunistas
Pero la poesía fue un desastre
Surrealismo de segunda mano
Decadentismo de tercera mano,
Tablas viejas devueltas por el mar.
Poesía adjetiva
Poesía nasal y gutural
Poesía arbitraria
Poesía copiada de los libros
Poesía basada
En la revolución de la palabra

"Libertad absoluta de expresión"

En circunstancias de que debe fundarse
En la revolución de las ideas.
Poesía de círculo vicioso
Para media docena de elegidos:

Hoy nos hacemos cruces preguntando
Para qué escribirían esas cosas
¿Para asustar al pequeño burgués?
¡Tiempo perdido miserablemente!
El pequeño burgués no reacciona
Sino cuando se trata del estómago.

¡Qué lo van a asustar con poesías!

La situación es ésta:
Mientras ellos estaban

Por una poesía del crepúsculo
Por una poesía de la noche
Nosotros propugnamos
La poesía del amanecer.
Este es nuestro mensaje,
Los resplandores de la poesía
Deben llegar a todos por igual
La poesía alcanza para todos.

Nada más, compañeros
Nosotros condenamos
—Y esto sí que lo digo con respeto—
La poesía de pequeño dios
La poesía de vaca sagrada
La poesía de toro furioso.

Contra la poesía de las nubes
Nosotros oponemos
La poesía de la tierra firme
—Cabeza fría, corazón caliente
Somos tierrafirmistas decididos
Contra la poesía de café
La poesía de la naturaleza
Contra la poesía de salón
La poesía de la plaza pública
La poesía de protesta social.

Los poetas bajaron del Olimpo.

Preguntas
a la hora
del té

Este señor desvaído parece
Una figura de un museo de cera;
Mira a través de los visillos rotos:
Qué vale más, ¿el oro o la belleza?,
¿Vale más el arroyo que se mueve
O la chépica fija a la ribera?
A lo lejos se oye una campana
Que abre una herida más, o que la cierra:
¿Es más real el agua de la fuente
O la muchacha que se mira en ella?
No se sabe, la gente se lo pasa
Construyendo castillos en la arena.
¿Es superior el vaso transparente
A la mano del hombre que lo crea?
Se respira una atmósfera cansada
De ceniza, de humo, de tristeza:

Lo que se vio una vez ya no se vuelve
A ver igual, dicen las hojas secas.
Hora del té, tostadas, margarina,
Todo envuelto en una especie de niebla.

El
túnel

Pasé una época de mi juventud en casa de unas tías
A raíz de la muerte de un señor íntimamente ligado a
    ellas
Cuyo fantasma las molestaba sin piedad
Haciéndoles imposible la vida.

En el principío yo me mantuve sordo a sus
    telegramas
A sus epístolas concebidas en un lenguaje de otra
    época
Llenas de alusiones mitológicas
Y de nombres propios desconocidos para mí
Varios de ellos pertenecientes a sabios de la antigüe-
    dad
A filósofos medievales de menor cuantía
A simples vecinos de la localidad que ellas habitaban.

Abandonar de buenas a primeras la universidad
Romper con los encantos de la vida galante
Interrumpirlo todo
Con el objeto de satisfacer los caprichos de tres an-
cianas histéricas
Llenas de toda clase de problemas personales
Resultaba, para una persona de mi carácter,
Un porvenir poco halagador
Una idea descabellada.

Cuatro años viví en El Túnel, sin embargo,
En comunidad con aquellas temibles damas
Cuatro años de martirio constante
De la mañana a la noche.
Las horas de regocijo que pasé debajo de los árboles
Tornáronse pronto en semanas de hastío
En meses de angustia que yo trataba de disimular al
máximo
Con el objeto de no despertar curiosidad en torno a mi
persona,
Tornáronse en años de ruina y de miseria
¡En siglos de prisión vividos por mi alma
En el interior de una botella de mesa!

Mi concepción espiritualista del mundo
Me situó ante los hechos en un plano de franca
inferioridad:
Yo lo veía todo a través de un prisma

En el fondo del cual las imágenes de mis tías se en-
trelazaban como hilos vivientes
Formando una especie de malla impenetrable
Que hería mi vista haciéndola cada vez más ineficaz.

Un joven de escasos recursos no se da cuenta de las
cosas.
El vive en una campana de vidrio que se llama Arte
Que se llama Lujuria, que se llama Ciencia
Tratando de establecer contacto con un mundo de
relaciones
Que sólo existen para él y para un pequeño grupo de
amigos.

Bajo los efectos de una especie de vapor de agua
Que se filtraba por el piso de la habitación
Inundando la atmósfera hasta hacerlo todo invisible
Yo pasaba los noches ante mi mesa de trabajo
Absorbido en la práctica de la escritura automática.

Pero para qué profundizar en estas materias desa-
gradables
Aquellas matronas se burlaron miserablemente de mí
Con sus falsas promesas, con sus extrañas fantasías
Con sus dolores sabiamente simulados
Lograron retenerme entre sus redes durante años
Obligándome tácitamente a trabajar para ellas
En faenas de agricultura

En compraventa de animales
Hasta que una noche, mirando por la cerradura
Me impuse que una de ellas
¡Mi tía paralítica!
Caminaba perfectamente sobre la punta de sus pier-
    nas
Y volví a la realidad con un sentimiento de los de-
    monios.

El
peregrino

Atención, señoras y señores, un momento de atención:
Volved un instante la cabeza hacia este lado de la
  república,
Olvidad por una noche vuestros asuntos personales,

El placer y el dolor pueden aguardar a la puerta:
Una voz se oye desde este lado de la república.
¡Atención, señoras y señores! ¡un momento de
  atención!

Un alma que ha estado embotellada durante años
En una especie de abismo sexual e intelecutal
Alimentándose escasamente por la nariz
Desea hacerse escuchar por ustedes.
Deseo que se me informe sobre algunas materias,
Necesito un poco de luz, el jardín se cubre de moscas,

175

Me encuentro en un desastroso estado mental,
Razono a mi manera;
Mientras digo estas cosas veo una bicicleta apoyada
en un muro,
Veo un puente
Y un automóvil que desaparece entre los edificios.

Ustedes se peinan, es cierto, ustedes andan a pie por
los jardines,
Debajo de la piel ustedes tienen otra piel,
Ustedes poseen un séptimo sentido
Que les permite entrar y salir automáticamente.
Pero yo soy un niño que llama a su madre detrás de la
rocas,
Soy un peregrino que hace saltar las piedras a la al-
tura de su nariz,
Un árbol que pide a gritos se le cubra de hojas.

Notas
de
viaje

Yo me mantuve alejado de mi puesto durante años.
Me dediqué a viajar, a cambiar impresiones con mis
    interlocutores,
Me dediqué a dormir;
Pero las escenas vividas en épocas anteriores se
    hacían presentes en mi memoria.
Durante el baile yo pensaba en cosas absurdas:
Pensaba en unas lechugas vistas el día anterior
Al pasar delante de la cocina,
Pensaba un sinnúmero de cosas fantásticas relacion-
    adas con mi familia;
Entretanto el barco ya había entrado al río,
Se abría paso a través de un banco de medusas.
Aquellas escenas fotográficas afectaban mi espíritu,

Me obligaban a encerrarme en mi camarote;
Comía a la fuerza, me rebelaba contra mí mismo,
Constituía un peligro permanente a bordo
Puesto que en cualquier momento podía salir con un
    contrasentido.

La
trampa

Por aquel tiempo yo rehuía las escenas demasiado
   misteriosas.
Como los enfermos del estómago que evitan las
   comidas pesadas,
Prefería quedarme en casa dilucidando algunas
   cuestiones
Referentes a la reproducción de las arañas,
Con cuyo objeto me recluía en el jardín
Y no aparecía en público hasta avanzadas horas de la
   noche;
O también en mangas de camisa, en actitud
   desafiante,
Solía lanzar iracundas miradas a la luna
Procurando evitar esos pensamientos atrabilarios

Que se pegan como pólipos al alma humana.
En la soledad poseía un dominio absoluto sobre mí
mismo,
Iba de un lado a otro con plena conciencia de mis actos
O me tendía entre las tablas de la bodega
A soñar, a idear mecanismos, a resolver pequeños
problemas de emergencia.
Aquellos eran los momentos en que ponía en práctica
mi célebre método onírico,
Que consiste en violentarse a sí mismo y soñar lo que
se desea,
En promover escenas preparadas de antemano con
participación del más allá.
De este modo lograba obtener informaciones
preciosas
Referentes a una serie de dudas que aquejan al ser:
Viajes al extranjero, confusiones eróticas, complejos
religiosos.
Pero todas las precauciones eran pocas
Puesto que por razones difíciles de precisar
Comenzaba a deslizarme automáticamente por una
especie de plano inclinado,
Como un globo que se desinfla mi alma perdía altura,
El instinto de conservación dejaba de funcionar
Y privado de mis prejuicios más esenciales
Caía fatalmente en la trampa del teléfono
Que como un abismo atrae a los objetos que lo rodean
Y con manos trémulas marcaba ese número maldito
Que aún suelo repetir automáticamente mientras
duermo.

De incertidumbre y de miseria eran aquellos segun-
dos
En que yo, como un esqueleto de pie delante de esa
mesa de infierno
Cubierta de una cretona amarilla,
Esperaba una respuesta desde el otro extremo del
mundo,
La otra mitad de mi ser prisionera en un hoyo.
Esos ruidos entrecortados del teléfono
Producían en mí el efecto de las máquinas perfor-
adoras de los dentistas,
Se incrustaban en mi alma como agujas lanzadas
desde lo alto
Hasta que, llegado el momento preciso,
Comenzaba a transpirar y a tartumudear febril-
mente.
Mi lengua parecida a un beefsteak de ternera
Se interponía entre mi ser y mi interlocutora
Como esas cortinas negras que nos separan de los
muertos.
Yo no deseaba sostener esas conversaciones dema-
siado íntimas
Que, sin embargo, yo mismo provocaba en forma
torpe
Con mi voz anhelante, cargada de electricidad.
Sentirme llamado por mi nombre de pila
En ese tono de familiaridad forzada
Me producía malestares difusos,
Perturbaciones locales de angustia que yo procuraba
conjurar

A través de un método rápido de preguntas y res-
puestas
Creando en ella un estado de efervescencia pseudo-
erótico
Que a la postre venía a repercutir en mí mismo
Bajo la forma de incipientes erecciones y de una sen-
sación de fracaso.
Entonces me reía a la fuerza cayendo después en un
estado de postración mental.
Aquellas charlas absurdas se prolongaban algunas
horas
Hasta que la dueña de la pensión aparecía
detrás del biombo
Interrumpiendo bruscamente aquel idilio estúpido,
Aquellas contorsiones de postulante al cielo
Y aquellas catástrofes tan deprimentes para mi es-
píritu
Que no terminaban completamente con colgar el
teléfono
Ya que, por lo general, quedábamos comprometidos
A vernos al día siguiente en una fuente de soda
O en la puerta de una iglesia de cuyo nombre no quiero
acordarme.

Recuerdos
de
juventud

Lo cierto es que yo iba de un lado a otro,
A veces chocaba con los árboles,
Chocaba con los mendigos,
Me abría paso a través de un bosque de sillas y mesas,
Con el alma en un hilo veía caer las grandes hojas.
Pero todo era inútil,
Cada vez me hundía más y más en una especie de
    jalea;
La gente se reía de mis arrebatos,
Los individuos se agitaban en sus butacas como algas
    movidas por las olas
Y las mujeres me dirigían miradas de odio
Haciéndome subir, haciéndome bajar,
Haciéndome llorar y reír en contra de mi voluntad

De todo esto resultó un sentimiento de asco,
Resultó una tempestad de frases incoherentes,

Amenazas, insultos, juramentos que no venían al
  caso,
Resultaron unos movimientos agotadores de caderas,
Aquellos bailes fúnebres
Que me dejaban sin respiración
Y que me impedían levantar cabeza durante días,
Durante noches.

Yo iba de un lado a otro, es verdad,
Mi alma flotaba en las calles
Pidiendo socorro, pidiendo un poco de ternura;
Con una hoja de papel y un lápiz yo entraba en los
  cementerios
Dispuesto a no dejarme engañar.
Daba vueltas y vueltas en torno al mismo asunto,
Observaba de cerca las cosas
O en un ataque de ira me arrancaba los cabellos.

De esa manera hice mi debut en las salas de clases,
Como un herido a bala me arrastré por los ateneos,
Crucé el umbral de las casas particulares,
Con el filo de la lengua traté de comunicarme con los
  espectadores:
Ellos leían el periódico
O desaparecían detrás de un taxi.

¡Adónde ir entonces!
A esas horas el cómercio estaba cerrado;
Yo pensaba en un trozo de cebolla visto durante la
  cena
Y en el abismo que nos separa de los otros abismos.

La
víbora

Durante largos años estuve condenado a adorar a una
    mujer despreciable
Sacrificarme por ella, sufrir humillaciones y burlas sin
    cuento,
Trabajar día y noche para alimentarla y vestirla,
Llevar a cabo algunos delitos, cometer algunas faltas,
A la luz de la luna realizar pequeños robos,
Falsificaciones de documentos comprometedores,
So pena de caer en descrédito ante sus ojos
    fascinantes.
En horas de comprensión solíamos concurrir a los
    parques
Y retratarnos juntos manejando una lancha a motor,
O nos íbamos a un café danzante
Donde nos entregábamos a un baile desenfrenado
Que se prolongaba hasta altas horas de la madrugada.

Largos años viví prisionero del encanto de aquella
mujer
Que solía presentarse a mi oficina completamente
desnuda
Ejecutando las contorsiones más difíciles de imaginar
Con el propósito de incorporar mi pobre alma a su
órbita
Y, sobre todo, para extorsionarme hasta el último
centavo.
Me prohibía estrictamente que me relacionase con mi
familia.
Mis amigos eran separados de mi mediante libelos
infamantes
Que la víbora hacía publicar en un diario de su
propiedad.
Apasionada hasta el dilirio no me daba un instante de
tregua,
Exigiéndome perentoriamente que besara su boca
Y que contestase sin dilación sus necias preguntas
Varias de ellas referentes a la eternidad y a la vida
futura
Temas que producían en mí un lamentable estado de
ánimo,
Zumbidos de oídos, entrecortadas náuseas, desvan-
ecimientos prematuros
Que ella sabía aprovechar con ese espíritu práctico
que la caracterizaba
Para vestirse rápidamente sin pérdida de tiempo
Y abandonar mi departamento dejándome con un
palmo de narices.

Esta situación se prolongó por más de cinco años.
Por temporadas vivíamos juntos en una pieza
    redonda
Que pagábamos a medias en un barrio de lujo cerca
    del cementerio.
(Algunas noches hubimos de interrumpir nuestra
    luna de miel
Para hacer frente a las ratas que se colaban por la
    ventana).

Llevaba la víbora un minucioso libro de cuentas
En el que anotaba hasta el más mínimo centavo que
    yo le pedía en préstamo;
No me permitía usar el cepillo de dientes que yo mis-
    mo le había regalado
Y me acusaba de haber arruinado su juventud:
Lanzando llamas por los ojos me emplazaba a com-
    parecer ante el juez
Y pagarle dentro de un plazo prudente parte de la
    deuda
Pues ella necesitaba ese dinero para continuar sus
    estudios
Entonces hube de salir a la calle y vivir de la caridad
    pública,
Dormir en los bancos de las plazas,
Donde fui encontrado muchas veces moribundo por la
    policía
Entre las primeras hojas del otoño.
Felizmente aquel estado de cosas no pasó más
    adelante,

Porque cierta vez en que yo me encontraba en una
   plaza también
Posando frente a una cámara fotográfica
Unas delicosas manos femeninas me vendaron de
   pronto la vista
Mientras una voz amada para mí me preguntaba
   quién soy yo.
Tú eres mi amor, respondí con serenidad.
¡Angel mío, dijo ella nerviosamente,
Permite que me siente en tus rodillas una vez más!
Entonces pude percatarme de que ella se presentaba
   ahora provista de un pequeño taparrabos.
Fue un encuentro memorable, aunque lleno de notas
   discordantes:
Me he comprado una parcela, no lejos del matadero,
   exclamó,
Allí pienso construir una especie de pirámide
En la que podamos pasar los últimos dias de nuestra
   vida.
Ya he terminado mis estudios, me he recibido de
   abogado,
Dispongo de un buen capital;
Dediquémonos a un negocio productivo, los dos, amor
   mío, agregó,
Lejos del mundo construyamos nuestro nido.
Basta de sandeces, repliqué, tus planes me inspiran
   desconfianza,
Piensa que de un momento a otro mi verdadera mujer
Puede dejarnos a todos en la miseria más espantosa.
Mi hijos han crecido ya, el tiempo ha transcurrido,

Me siento profundamente agotado, déjame reposar
  un instante,
Tráeme un poco de agua, mujer,
Consígueme algo de comer en alguna parte,
Estoy muerto de hambre,
No puedo trabajar más para ti,
Todo ha terminado entre nosotros.

Bibliography

Alegría, Fernando. "Nicanor Parra, el anti-poeta," *CuA*, XIX, no. 3 (1960), 209-220.

Alonso, Amado. *Poesía y estilo de Pablo Neruda: Interpretación de una poesía hermética*. 3a ed. Buenos Aires: Editorial Sudamericana, 1966.

Aristophanes. *Lysistrata, The Birds, The Clouds*. Chicago: Henry Regnery Co., 1948.

Baudelaire, Charles. *The Essence of Laughter and Other Essays, Journals and Letters*. Ed. Peter Quennel. New York: Meridian Books, 1956.

Bousoño, Carlos. *Teoría de la expresión poética. Hacia una explicación del fenómeno lírico a través de textos españoles*. 3a ed. aum. Madrid: Editorial Gredos, 1962.

Davison, Ned J. "Parra, Nicanor. *La cueca larga y otros poemas.*" *HispW*, XLIX, no. 3 (1966).

191

Franco, Jean. *The Modern Culture of Latin America. Society and the Artist.* Rev. ed. Baltimore: Penguin Books, 1970.

García, Pablo. "Contrafigura de Nicanor Parra." *A*, CXIX (1955) 150-163.

Gottlieb, Marlene. "The Poetry of Nicanor Parra." Diss. Columbia University, 1971.

Hamburger, Michael. *The Truth of Poetry. Tensions in Modern Poetry from Baudelaire to the 1960s.* New York: Harcourt Brace Jovanovich, 1969.

Hastings, James, ed. *Encyclopedia of Religion and Ethics.* vols. I, VII, VIII. New York: Charles Scribner's Sons, n.d.

Hays, H.R., tr. and introd. *Selected Poems* by Bertolt Brecht. New York: Grove Press, 1959.

Henderson, Harold G., ed. and tr. *An Introduction to Haiku: An Anthology of Poems and Poets from Basho to Shiki.* New York: Anchor Books, 1958.

Hersh, Burton. "The Man in the Ironic Mask." *Horizon*, IV, no. 5 (May 1962) 35-41.

Lerzundi, Patricio. "In Defense of Antipoetry. An Interview with Nicanor Parra." Tr. Tom J. Lewis. *Review* (Winter 1971/Spring 1972) 65-72.

Lihn, Enrique. "Introducción a la poesía de Nicanor Parra. Estudio, datos biográficos y selección." *AUCh*, CIX (1951) 276-286.

Lindo, Hugo. "Nicanor, antipoeta." *RepAm* (marzo 1958), 44-45.

Machado de Arnao, Luz. "Nicanor Parra, *La cueca larga y otros poemas.*" *Universal Car.* (24 agosto, 1965).

Montes, Hugo and Rodríguez, Mario. *Nicanor Parra y la poesía de lo cotidiano.* Santiago de Chile: Editorial de Pacífico, S. A., 1970.

Morales T., Leonidas, *La poesía de Nicanor Parra.* Santiago de Chile: Universidad Austral de Chile & Editorial Andrés Bello, 1972.

Murray, Gilbert. *The Literature of Ancient Greece.* 3rd ed. Chicago: University of Chicago Press, 1956.

Neruda, Pablo and Parra, Nicanor. *Discursos.* Santiago de Chile: Editorial Nascimento, 1962.

Ortega, Julio. "Nicanor Parra y las paradojas." *MNuP*, no. 11 (1967) 90-91.

Parra, Nicanor. *Artefactos.* Santiago de Chile: Universidad Católica de Chile, 1972.

———. *Canciones rusas.* Santiago de Chile: Editorial Universitaria, 1967.

———. and Pablo Neruda. *Discursos.* Santiago de Chile: Editorial Nascimento, 1962.

———. *Emergency Poems.* Tr. Miller Williams. New York: New Directions, 1972.

———. *La cueca larga y otros poemas.* ed. and prol. Margarita Aguirre and Juan Agustín Palazuelos. Buenos Aires: Editorial Universitaria, 1964.

———. *Obra gruesa.* Santiago de chile: Editorial Universitaria, 1969.

———. *Poemas y antipoemas*, 3a ed. Santiago de Chile: Editorial Universitaria, 1964.

———. *Poems and Antipoems.* Ed. Miller Williams. New York: New Directions, 1967.

———. "Problems/Poems." [unpublished].

———. "Routine and Emergency Poems" [unpublished].

———. *Versos de salón.* Santiago de Chile: Editorial Nascimento, 1962.

Pears, David. *Ludwig Wittgenstein.* New York: The Viking Press, Inc., 1970.

Perry, Janet H., ed. *The Heath Anthology of Spanish Poetry.* Boston: D. C. Heath and Company, n.d.

Pineda, Rafael. "Nicanor Parra: *Poems and Antipoems.*" *RNC*, XXIX, no. 182 (1967) 121-122.

Pound, Ezra. *ABC of Reading.* 1934. New York: New Directions rpt., 1960.

Rodríguez Monegal, Emir. "Encuentros con Nicanor Parra." *MuN.* no. 23 (mayo 1968) 75-83.

———. *El viajero inmóvil. Introducción a Pablo Neruda.* Buenos Aires: Editorial Losada, 1966.

Rodríguez Rivera, Guillermo, prol. *Poemas de Nicanor Parra.* Colección de literatura latinoamericana. Habana: Casa de las Americas, 1969 [distributed in mimeographed sheets without pagination by Parra to his seminar at New York University, 1971].

Rossler, Osvaldo. "*Obra gruesa* por Nicanor Parra." *Nac.* (5 octubre, 1969).

Schopf, Federico. "La escritura de la semejanza en Nicanor Parra." *RCL*, nos. 2 and 3 (primavera 1970) 43-142.

de la Selva, Mauricio. "Nicanor Parra, *La cueca larga y otros poemas.*" *CuA*, XXV, no. 2 (1966), 270-272.

Silva Castro, Raul. "*Antipoemas* por Nicanor Parra." *Merc*, Santiago de Chile (29 abril 1960).

Skarmeta, Antonio. "El apogeo del antipoeta." *Ercilla* (1971), 34-39. This issue is not available for consultation.

Teillier, Jorge. "*La cueca larga*, poemas de Nicanor Parra." *AUCh*, CXVI, no. 11 (1958), 7.

Thilly, Frank. *A History of Philosophy*. Rev. Ledger Wood. New York: Henry Holt and Company, Inc., 1951.

Tuve, Rosemond. *Elizabethan and Metaphysical Imagery: Renaissance Poetic and Twentieth-Century Critics*. Chicago: The University of Chicago Press, 1961.

Valente, Ignacio. "El sentido religioso de los antipoemas." *Merc*. Santiago de Chile (27 agosto, 1967).

Zardoya, Concha. *Poesía española contemporánea. Estudios temáticos y estilísticos*. Madrid: Ediciones Guadarrama, 1961.

P. C. "Poesía chilena de Huidobro a Parra." *Nac*. (18 marzo, 1969).

Unsigned. "Nicanor Parra, *Versos de salón.*" *Día Mex.*, no. 2 (1965) 36.

Index